THE CRISIS OF CARING

P&R
PUBLISHING
P.O. BOX 817 • PHILLIPSBURG • NEW JERSEY 08865-0817

The Crisis of Caring:
Recovering the Meaning of True Fellowship

(Originally published as *True Fellowship)*

First printing, paperback edition 1987

Manufactured in the United States of America

Library of Congress Cataloging-in-Publication Data

Bridges, Jerry.
[True fellowship]
The crisis of caring : recovering the meaning of true fellowship / Jerry Bridges.
p. cm.
Originally published: True fellowship. Colorado Springs, Colo. : NavPress, c1985, in series: The Christian character library.
Includes bibliographical references.
ISBN 0-87552-110-X (pbk.)
1. Fellowship—Religious aspects—Christianity. I. Title.
BV4517.5.B75 1992
262—dc20 92-14842

Contents

To the dear friends who,
through their prayer and financial support,
are partners with me in the ministry—
this book is gratefully dedicated.

In all my prayers for all of you,
I always pray with joy because
of your partnership *(koinōnia)*
in the gospel from the first day
until now.

Philippians 1:4-5

Preface

There is a crisis of caring in the Church of Jesus Christ today. Many Christians readily identify with David's lament, "No one is concerned for me. . . . no one cares for my life" (Psalm 142:4). We are all so busy, absorbed in our own responsibilities and insulated from one another. We pass each other like ships in the night, uttering a friendly but empty, "Hi, how're you doing?" and hearing an equally hollow response, "Oh, fine, how're you?" We'd be shocked if someone replied, "Would you really like to know?"

What's behind all this superficial friendliness and these empty relationships? Why is there a crisis of caring in the Church? There are probably several reasons, but one of the most crucial is this:

We believers today do not know, either intellectually or experientially, the meaning of true fellowship as it was practiced in the early Church and passed on to us by the writers of the New Testament.

Several years ago a friend of mine asked me to speak at a conference he was directing on the subject of *koinōnia,* which is the Greek word for fellowship. I responded, "Oh, you want me to speak on *fellowship*?" "No," he replied. "I want you to speak on koinonia. The word 'fellowship' has become so watered down in our Christian culture that it no longer conveys the same meaning it did in New Testament times."

I accepted his challenge by embarking on an in-depth study of the New Testament usage of *koinōnia*. What did I find out? To put it simply, I was amazed. Up to that time I had considered my idea of New Testament fellowship to be more biblical than the typical cultural, coffee-drinking concept of fellowship. But I soon learned that my own concept was far more limited than the Bible's, and thus defective.

As I grew in my understanding of the rich, full meaning of fellowship as it was practiced in the early Church, my attitude and my sense of responsibility toward other believers began to change. I was convinced that I had a lot of growing to do. I'm still struggling to catch up in practical application with all the wonderful truths I learned from that study.

It is my prayer that sharing the truths of New Testament fellowship with the readers of this book will both sharpen my own obedience and expose other believers to the wonders of the biblical practice of koinonia.

I extend my appreciation to a number of people who have contributed in one way or another to the writing of this book. First, there is my friend and fellow staff member of The Navigators, Jim Morris, who first challenged me to study and teach on the subject of koinonia. Then, the editorial staff of NavPress provided often-needed encouragement, as well as professional editing skill. Deborah Holmen, with her gracious, serving spirit, patiently typed—and in many instances retyped several times—all the pages of the manuscript. Good friends John Mahon and Paul Moede read several key chapters and offered valuable suggestions. Finally, my wife, Eleanor, and numerous other friends prayed for me through those frequently frustrating times when the right words just didn't seem to come. The process of writing this book has thus been a concrete expression of what biblical fellowship is meant to be.

1
What Is Fellowship?

THEY DEVOTED THEMSELVES
TO THE APOSTLES' TEACHING
AND TO THE FELLOWSHIP,
TO THE BREAKING OF BREAD
AND TO PRAYER.

Acts 2:42

The very first account of the New Testament Church highlights the importance of fellowship. Luke described this Body of believers, newly formed on the day of Pentecost, as people "devoted to the apostles' teaching and to the fellowship, to the breaking of bread and to prayer" (Acts 2:42).

We're not too surprised that Luke mentions their attention to the apostles' teaching. After all, isn't one of the main purposes of a church service to listen to the Word of God taught by men ordained of God? And we would also expect these brand-new believers to devote themselves to prayer, for the Word of God and prayer are the two primary God-given means for building us up in the Christian faith. But what about this matter of fellowship? Luke says they "devoted themselves . . . to the fellowship." They didn't just *have* fellowship; they *devoted* themselves to it! They gave it a priority in their lives along with prayer and hearing the Word taught.

Then consider what the Apostle John wrote to fellow Christians in 1 John 1:3: "We proclaim to you what we have seen and heard, so that you also may have fellowship with us." May have fellowship with us? Wasn't it Christian growth John was concerned about? Didn't he want these believers to have assurance of their salvation and to walk in obedience to God's commands? Why was he so concerned about fellowship?

Now consider us—the modern-day Christians. We, too, are concerned about fellowship. Many local churches like yours and mine even have a room called "fellowship hall." In our church it's used for a variety of purposes, but its position adjacent to the church kitchen reveals its primary use. It is a place where "food and fellowship" is enjoyed on many occasions. We all look forward to those times of passing pleasantries over coffee and doughnuts on Sunday morning, or sampling Mrs. Smith's famous cherry pie at the potluck dinner during the church's annual missions conference.

Christian student ministries on campuses are also interested in fellowship. An event is often described as "a time of food, fun, and fellowship." I have even heard of students being warned about having too much fellowship, so it must be a popular activity. Yes, we modern-day Christians, just like those early believers from the day of Pentecost, are eager to devote ourselves to fellowship. There is only one problem: We have lost sight of the biblical meaning of fellowship. We are devoting ourselves to the wrong thing.

Fellowship, as it is described for us in the Bible, is much more than Christian social activity. It is more than enjoying food together, or playing games in a Christian atmosphere, or chatting with one another about the events of the past week. This doesn't mean that there is no place for such activities. It is just that they are not true fellowship. They may, if entered into for the right purpose, contribute to fellowship, but in and of themselves they are not fellowship.

Many Christians have recognized that there is a deeper and richer meaning to the biblical concept of fellowship. They are not content with the idea of mere social activity. Among these people it is not unusual to hear someone say, "Let's get together for some fellowship." What these people usually mean is, "Let's get together to share with each other from the Bible and pray together." Or perhaps these people bring each other up to date on how God has been working in each of their lives. These certainly are important spiritual activities, and they are certainly a part of biblical fellowship. Yet even these activities fail to capture the rich, full meaning of the fellowship described to us in the New Testament.

Once we discover the full meaning of New Testament fellowship, we'll understand why Luke spoke approvingly of the fact that those Pentecost believers devoted themselves to it. We'll also understand why John was so eager for his readers to have fellowship with him. And we will see why the idea of fellowship as a term for Christian social activity utterly empties the word of its New Testament meaning.

The Greek word for fellowship is *koinōnia*. It is translated several ways in the New Testament: for example, "participation," "partnership," "sharing," and, of course, "fellowship." These various uses of koinonia convey two related meanings: (1) *to share together* in the sense of joint participation or partnership, and (2) *to share with* in the sense of giving what we have to others.

Relationship

Each of these two meanings can be further divided under two subheadings. To share together in the sense of joint participation refers primarily to a *relationship* that we as believers have in Christ. This is the fellowship to which John called his readers: "What we have seen and heard we declare to you, so that you and we together may share in a common life, that life which we share with the Father and his Son Jesus Christ" (1 John 1:3, *New English Bible*). Fellowship is sharing a common life with other believers, a life that we together share with God the Father and God the Son. *It is a relationship, not an activity.*

Those first Christians of Acts 2 were not devoting themselves to social activities but to a relationship—a relationship that consisted of sharing together the very life of God through the indwelling of the Holy Spirit. They understood that they had entered this relationship by faith in Jesus Christ, not by joining an organization. And they realized that their fellowship with God logically brought them into fellowship with one another. Through their union with Christ they were formed into a spiritually organic *community*. They were living stones being built into a spiritual house (1 Peter 2:5), fellow members of the Body of Christ. As William Hendriksen said, "Koinonia, then, is basically a community-relationship."[1] It is not primarily an activity; it is a relationship.

If we miss the fact that koinonia denotes first of all a community relationship in Christ among all believers, then we miss the most significant aspect of true biblical fellowship. We must grasp the idea that fellowship means belonging to one another in the Body of Christ, along with all the privileges and responsibilities that such a relationship entails.

Partnership

Koinonia also means to share together in the sense of partnership. Both classical Greek writers and New Testament writers used *koinōnia* to refer to a business partnership. Plato spoke of the dissolution of a *koinōnia*—a business partnership.[2] Luke used a form of *koinōnia* to refer to the partnership of Peter with James and John in the fishing business (Luke 5:10).

In the spiritual realm, Paul regarded himself as a partner with his dear friend Philemon, and he thanked God for the Philippian believers' partnership in the gospel (Philemon 17, Philippians 1:5). And when Paul went to Jerusalem to dispute with the legalists over the necessity of circumcision, he said, "James, Cephas, and John . . . accepted Barnabas and myself as partners" (Galatians 2:9, NEB). The concept of fellowship as a spiritual partnership is firmly embedded in the New Testament use of koinonia.

Whereas relationship describes believers as a community, partnership describes them as the principals of an enterprise. A business partnership is always formed in order to attain an objective, such as providing a service to the public at a profit for the partners. In the same way, the concept of a spiritual partnership implies that it is created with the objective of glorifying God. Just as all believers are united together in a community relationship, so we are all united together in a partnership formed to glorify God. God is glorified when Christians grow in Christlikeness and when unbelievers are brought into His Kingdom. Biblical fellowship, then, incorporates this idea of an active partnership in the promotion of the gospel and the building up of believers.

Communion with others

The second primary meaning of New Testament koinonia is to share with others what we have. Just as *sharing together* has two sub-meanings (relationship and partnership), so *sharing with* has two sub-meanings. The first of these can be called *communion* with one another. Although we usually use the word communion as a term for the Lord's

Supper, it is here used to mean communicating intimately or sharing with one another on a close personal and spiritual level. It may be the mutual sharing among believers of what God has taught them from the Scriptures, or it may be a word of encouragement from one believer to another. The key element is that the subject matter is focused on God as well as on His Word and His works. As J.I. Packer said, "It is, first, a sharing with our fellow-believers the things that God has made known to us about himself, in hope that we may thus help them to know him better and so enrich their fellowship with him."[3] This, of course, is what we usually have in mind when we say, "Let's have some fellowship together."

According to Acts 2:5-11, the first believers who were gathered into the Church on the day of Pentecost came from "every nation under heaven." Prior to their conversion they would have related to one another like billiard balls, constantly colliding and bouncing off one another. But immediately after coming into the community relationship of the Body of Christ, they began to experience koinonia and to value its effect in their lives. The *New English Bible* says in Acts 2:42, "They met constantly to hear the apostles teach, and to share the common life." The *New International Version* says, "They devoted themselves . . . to the fellowship." They couldn't get enough teaching, fellowship, and prayer.

Those first Christians from the day of Pentecost were all Jews. They were steeped in the Old Testament Scriptures, but as they listened to the apostles' teaching and were enlightened by the Holy Spirit, they began to see those Scriptures in a new way. They were daily gaining a new understanding of them. And as they individually learned from the apostles' teaching, they shared with one another what they were learning. This is fellowship: sharing with one another what God is teaching through the Scriptures.

How different is our present-day concept of fellowship? Take those typical times of "coffee fellowship." We discuss everything else *except* the Scriptures. We talk about our jobs, our studies, our favorite sports teams, the weather—almost anything except what God is teaching us from His Word and through His workings in our lives. If we are to regain the New Testament concept of fellowship, we must learn to get beyond the temporal issues of the day and begin to share with each other on a level that will enhance our spiritual relationships with one another and with God.

Sharing material possessions

As we examine the account of these early believers' attitudes, however, we see that they did not limit their concept of koinonia to *sharing with* one another only spiritual things. They also shared their material possessions with those in need (Acts 2:44-45).

One of the most common usages of koinonia in the New Testament is this sense of sharing material resources with others. For example, Paul urges us to "share with God's people who are in need" (Romans 12:13). In 2 Corinthians 9:13, he speaks of "your generosity in sharing with [others]." The writer of Hebrews urges us to "not forget to do good and to share with others" (Hebrews 13:16). The word "share" in these passages is a translation of *koinōnia* in either its noun or verb form. A willingness to share our possessions with one another is a very important aspect of true biblical fellowship.

Sharing our possessions with others should be a natural consequence of our realization that biblical fellowship denotes both a relationship *and* a partnership. Paul said that all parts of the Body should have concern for one another (1 Corinthians 12:25-26). We will be concerned for the needs of others in the Body only to the extent that we see fellowship as primarily a mutual relationship in Christ among members of the same spiritual organism. The fellowship of sharing with those in need is more than just showing compassion or benevolence to those in need. Even unbelievers do that. The fellowship of sharing possessions within the Body is a tangible recognition that we are in a community relationship with one another and that when one member of the community suffers, we all suffer together. When a parent meets a need of one of his children, we do not think of that act as an expression of benevolence but as an expression of relationship. It is both his privilege and his duty to meet that need because he is the parent. In the same manner, believers have both a privilege and a duty to share with each other as fellow members of the same Body.

Similarly, in a partnership the partners share

in both the income and the expenses, both the assets and the liabilities of the partnership. No one ever establishes a business partnership where one partner takes all the income and another pays all the bills. They share alike in both the positive and the negative. It should be the same way in the fellowship of the Church. Because we are partners in the gospel, we need to *share* with one another, realizing that we are not owners but only stewards of the possessions God has entrusted (not given, but entrusted) to us.

We see the application of this principle of partnership in 2 Corinthians 8:13-14: "Our desire is not that others might be relieved while you are hard pressed, but that there might be equality. At the present time your plenty will supply what they need, so that in turn their plenty will supply what you need." Paul envisioned a continual flow of believers' possessions toward those who have needs. This is an outworking of koinonia, an important expression of true fellowship.

Paul was urging the Corinthian believers to have *fellowship* with Christians they had never even met and never would meet: the poor among the believers in Jerusalem. They were not going to have coffee and doughnuts together with these people in need; they were going to dig down into their pockets to help meet the needs of these believers who shared together with them a common life in Christ.

In this first chapter we have seen that koinonia is used in the New Testament to express four different but related dimensions of fellowship:

- Community relationship
- Partnership
- Communion
- Sharing material possessions.

The first two are dimensions of fellowship as *sharing together*; the second two, as *sharing with one another*. It is because we share together a common life in Christ that we are called on to share with one another whatever we have, both spiritual and material resources.

We will explore the implications of these four expressions of fellowship in subsequent chapters. Before we do, however, we will look at the foundation for our fellowship with one another: *fellowship with God*. It is important that we take time to lay this foundation, because we cannot have meaningful fellowship with one another unless we are individually experiencing vital fellowship with God.

Notes

1. William Hendriksen, *Exposition of Philippians* (Grand Rapids: Baker Book House, 1962), page 94.
2. Hendriksen, page 93.
3. J.I. Packer, *God's Words* (Downers Grove, IL: InterVarsity Press, 1981), page 195.

2
Union with God

GOD, WHO HAS CALLED YOU INTO FELLOWSHIP WITH HIS SON JESUS CHRIST OUR LORD, IS FAITHFUL.

1 Corinthians 1:9

What does the word *relationship* mean to you? Does it indicate an objective fact or a subjective experience? For example, if I say, "I have a good relationship with my son," what do I mean? Obviously I am referring to a positive state of affairs that exists between us; I am speaking of our subjective experience. We use "relationship" this way all the time. We speak of the importance of relationships in our campus ministry groups, our local churches, and our home Bible studies. In such cases we are emphasizing the importance of getting to know one another, loving and accepting one another, and encouraging one another. All these relational actions speak of our experience with each other in our day-to-day lives.

But the most basic meaning of relationship has to do with an objective fact. The dictionary defines relationship as the condition or fact of being related, as in a marriage relationship. When a man and woman marry, they enter into a relationship. As the years pass, their relationship may be good or bad. But whatever their experience, the fact remains that they do have a certain kind of relationship with one another.

In Chapter 1 we saw that koinonia expresses, first of all, the meaning of relationship in this objective manner. All believers are related to one another in the sense that we all share together a common life in Christ. Our experiential relationships with one another grow out of our objective relationship. Only those who are *in* fellowship with one another (objective fact) can *have* fellowship with one another (subjective experience).

Now just as this objective fact of relationship is the most basic concept of fellowship among believers, so it is also the most basic concept of fellowship with God. We must first have an objective, living relationship with God before we can enjoy an experiential relationship with Him. We must be united to Christ by saving faith before we can have fellowship with Him on a daily basis.

True fellowship embraces both the objective and the experiential aspects of our relationship with God. The old writers of several generations ago referred to these two aspects of fellowship as *union* and *communion* with God. When we consider the subject of fellowship with God, we should look at both aspects: the objective and the experiential. Only as we understand our objective union with Christ will we be able to enter fully into the experiential joys of communion with Him.

Sharing Christ's life

Paul states in 1 Corinthians 1:9, "God, who has called you into fellowship with his Son Jesus Christ our Lord, is faithful." Many of us have used this verse as a biblical basis for a morning quiet time, a time when believers may have regular communion with God. We point out to new believers this fantastic privilege of being called by God to have such special communion with His Son Jesus Christ. While this is indeed part of what Paul is saying, it is not the main thrust of his statement. In this passage (verses 8-9), Paul is actually grounding the assurance of the Corinthians' salvation at the coming day of Christ in the faithfulness of God, who called them into a relationship with Christ.

Regarding this passage, F.W. Grosheide wrote, "The word *fellowship* . . . is the clue to the understanding of *unreprovable* ["blameless" in the NIV] in verse 8. How is it possible that the Corinthians will be unreprovable in the day of Christ? Because they stand in relation to Him and share in the fruits of His work."[1] Or as Matthew Henry put it, "He who hath brought us into near and dear relation to Christ, into sweet and intimate communion with Christ, is faithful; he may be trusted with our dearest concerns."[2] Similarly, Charles Hodge wrote on this passage, "*Fellowship* includes union and communion. The original word (*koinōnia*) signifies participation. . . . We are called to be partakers of Christ; partakers of his life, as members of his body."[3]

Thus, while the word "fellowship" as used in 1 Corinthians 1:9 includes both union and communion with Christ, it is the *union*, the objective relation with Him, that is primarily in view. Through faith in Christ, we are members of His Body. The term "His Body" does not signify merely ownership, as we might say in the expression "his house" or "his car." Rather, it signifies union or an actual attachment, as in the expression "his hand" or "his heart."

Your hand and your heart do not merely belong to you in the sense of ownership. They are an integral part of you. In the same way, we, the members of Christ's Body, not only belong to Him (though that in itself is certainly true), but we are also spiritually a part of Him, "for we are members of his body" (Ephesians 5:30). He is our life and we are His Body, receiving every iota of our spiritual lives from Him.

The Apostle John also sees fellowship with God primarily in terms of an objective relationship. He states, "What we have seen and heard we declare to you, so that you and we together may *share in a common life*, that *life which we share* with the Father and his Son Jesus Christ. . . . If we claim to be *sharing in his life* while we walk in the dark, our words and our lives are a lie; but if we walk in the light as he himself is in the light, then we *share together a common life*, and we are being cleansed from every sin by the blood of Jesus his

Son" (1 John 1:3,6-7, NEB, italics added).

The four italicized phrases in this quotation are all translations of the Greek word *koinōnia.* It is apparent that John is focusing on the relationship he has with God and that he wants his readers to have the same kind of vital relationship.

Many of us are accustomed to thinking of the concept of fellowship used in 1 Corinthians 1:9 and 1 John 1:3,6-7 only in terms of communion with Christ through a daily quiet time, Scripture meditation, and prayer. Therefore, at the risk of belaboring my point, I want to emphasize again that the primary idea in these passages is that of *union* with Christ. And so I quote again from other authorities.

W. E. Vine, author of the well-known *Vine's Expository Dictionary of New Testament Words,* says on 1 John 1:3, "The life [of Christ] was manifested not merely to reveal God but to bring the redeemed into *relationship* with Him." Commenting on verse 6, Vine says, "To walk in the light we must be *partakers* of His nature." And then on verse 7, he says, "There is first *union* and then *communion.* There cannot be the latter without the former" (italics added).[4]

New Testament scholar Donald W. Burdick says, "The breadth of [*koinōnia's*] usage is to be seen in the fact that New Testament *koinōnia* is first of all fellowship with God. *To be a Christian is the same as being in fellowship with Him*" [italics added].[5] It is obvious that Professor Burdick is speaking of an objective relationship with God that is true of all Christians.

I. Howard Marshall of the University of Aberdeen, Scotland, says on 1 John 1:3, "Here the thought of union with God is uppermost."[6]

Now what is the point of all this? Why belabor the fact that koinonia denotes first of all relationship with God in these passages of Scripture? Because it is important for us to realize that, by God's grace, *all believers share in the very life of Christ Himself!* As wonderful as it is to realize that God calls us to have communion with Him each day, it is far more wonderful to know that He has called us to actually share in the life of His Son Jesus Christ.

One of the Apostle Paul's favorite expressions in his letters was the phrase "in Christ," by which he referred to that vital union that exists between the believer and Christ. It is this union that is symbolized by Jesus' analogy of the vine and the branches and by Paul's analogy of the head and the body. Both of these illustrations are intended to teach that the believer is united to Christ in such a way that he participates in all the virtue and power residing in the risen and glorified Christ. Just as the branch shares the life of the vine and just as the body shares the life of the head, so the believer shares the life of Christ because he is "in Him."

Robert Haldane, an early nineteenth-century writer of a classic commentary on Romans, put it this way:

> He [the believer] is now united to Him who has the inexhaustible fulness of the Spirit, and he

> cannot fail to participate in the spirit of holiness which dwells without measure in his glorious Head. It is impossible that the streams can be dried up when the fountain continues to flow; and it is equally impossible for the members not to share in the same holiness which dwells so abundantly in the Head. As the branch, when united to the living vine, necessarily partakes of its life and fatness, so the sinner, when united to Christ, must receive an abundant supply of sanctifying grace out of His immeasurable fulness.[7]

Where do we Christians get the power we need to live the Christian life? All of us will acknowledge that the power comes from the Lord Jesus Christ. We are to "be strong in the Lord and in his mighty power" (Ephesians 6:10). But *how* do we obtain this power? The answer is *through our union with Him.* We have been called to share in His very life. God did not call us into *association* with Christ but into *union* with Him, into an actual sharing of His all-powerful life.

It was several years after I became a Christian that I began to understand the significance of our union with Christ and to consciously experience the reality of that union in my daily life. I knew Christ as my Savior, and I also knew how to practice the basic essentials of the Christian life. I had a regular quiet time, led a Bible study, memorized Scripture, shared the gospel with others, and sought to live an obedient Christian life. I even memorized many verses of Scripture that contained the phrase "in Christ," and yet I did not realize the significance of that marvelous expression. My concept of praying for the power to live the Christian life was somewhat akin to a college student writing home for more money: I might get it and I might not. I felt destitute—like a spiritual pauper.

Then one day I grasped the significance of what Paul meant when he said that we are *in Christ*. The Holy Spirit helped me realize that I was a branch intimately and vitally joined to the vine—not just tacked on to the vine, but actually a part of it. I understood that just as the life of that vine flows naturally into the branch, so the life of Jesus Christ flows naturally into me.

I later realized that every expression of the Christian life in and through me since the day of my conversion was the result of my union with Christ and, consequently, of His life at work in me. Every desire to read the Bible and to do God's will, every manifestation of the fruit of the Spirit, be it ever so small, was the living result of my being in Christ.

Our union with Christ is an objective fact that is true whether we realize it or not. It is also true that, to a degree, we experience the fruit of that union apart from any conscious effort on our part. For example, at conversion we begin to experience a degree of spiritual enlightenment and understanding of the Scriptures, a degree of change in our desires and affections, and some inclination of our wills to live lives pleasing to God. It is true that just as the life of the vine flows naturally into the branch, so the life of Jesus Christ flows naturally into you and me, causing these changes in our lives.

Abiding in Christ

But the analogies of the branch on the vine and the members of the body should not be pressed so far as to give the impression that we are passive in our union with Christ. Jesus told us in the analogy of the vine and the branches to remain, or to abide, in Him (John 15:4-5). Paul likewise said, "Continue to live in him, rooted and built up in him, strengthened in the faith" (Colossians 2:6-7). We are to remain in Christ, continuing to live in Him. Clearly this act of continuing to abide is something we are commanded to do.

We must renounce all confidence in our own wisdom, power, and merit, instead looking entirely to Christ for what we need to live the Christian life. But what makes the looking to Him effective and fruitful is the fundamental fact that we *are* in Him. To use an imaginary illustration, a branch can draw no life from the vine unless it is an integral part of that vine. It does no good to nail an unattached branch to the vine; there is no life-giving connection. But those branches that are an integral part of the vine share in the life of the vine.

This is what God has done in calling us into fellowship with His Son Jesus Christ. He has brought us into a vital relationship with Christ that is as intimate as the relationship of the branch to the vine and the body to the head. He has made us to share in the very life of Christ Himself. In doing so, God has made us to be *partakers* (*koinōnoi*) of the divine nature (2 Peter 1:4).

In the Preface, I referred to the four-spoked Wheel that The Navigators use to illustrate the most basic elements of the Christian life. The hub of that Wheel represents Christ at the center of the Christian life. In recent years we have tended to stress Christ at the center of the Wheel as signifying the lordship of Jesus Christ in the life of a Christian. Although this is certainly a vital truth that needs emphasis, it has not been the historic emphasis of the hub. Rather, the hub signifies Christ as the source of power of the Christian life. Just as the power of a wheel comes from its hub through the spokes to turn the rim, the power for the Christian life comes from Jesus Christ through such means as the Word of God and prayer. An illustration of the Wheel designed by Dawson Trotman about 1930 has this statement on it: "Christ supplies the power in a Christian life, as does the hub in the mechanism of a wheel in action." This is followed by a quote from John 15:5: "I am the vine, ye are the branches. Without Me ye can do nothing."[8]

Nowadays as we teach the Wheel, we tend to focus on the spokes: the things we must *do,* such as getting into the Word and praying. In so doing, we tend to neglect a proper emphasis on the hub, Jesus Christ, who is, after all, the source of the power for the Christian life. It is not the Word of God itself or even prayer that supplies the power and grace to live the Christian life; it is Christ who is our life (Colossians 3:4). The Word of God and prayer are the primary means by which the Holy Spirit mediates Christ's life to us. We must never so emphasize the spokes of the Wheel, which are God's channels of grace, that we lose sight of the hub, Jesus Christ, who is the source of our life.

We must actively "abide in Christ"; that is, we must look to Him by faith to sustain us, nurture us, and provide all that we need to live a life pleasing to God and worthy of Him. When we come to Christ for salvation, we renounce any confidence in ourselves, placing our trust entirely in Him. In the same way, as we live the Christian life we should continue to renounce any confidence in ourselves, placing our trust entirely in Him. But this does not mean we should become passive in a "let go and let God" approach to the Christian life. Rather, we are called to a dependence on Christ, as well as a dependence on the Holy Spirit, whose work it is to mediate the life of Christ to us, enabling us to live the kind of lives that are pleasing to God.

Four ways to live

There are basically four ways to live the Christian life. The first way is to attempt to do it entirely on our own, by our own effort and willpower. This way is doomed to failure. Jesus stated very plainly, "Apart from me you can do nothing" (John 15:5). If we attempt such a solo effort, some meager expressions of the life of Christ will remain in us, for, after all, we are still in union with Him. But in our daily spiritual life we will experience mostly failure, frustration, and, very likely, unsatisfactory relationships with other people. The fruit of the Spirit—love, joy, peace, patience, kindness, etc.—will hardly be visible. Instead of growing vigorously in our lives, those gracious qualities will be stunted and withered. We may have lots of Christian activity and even apparent Christian success, but we will possess little genuine Spirit-produced fruit. Most of us have probably tried this solo approach to the Christian life and found it wanting.

The second way to live the Christian life is frequently a reaction to the first. Having experienced the futility of the self-effort way, we go to the other extreme, deciding to do nothing at all. We just "turn it all over to the Lord" and allow Him to live His life through us. We decide, perhaps because we have heard or read it some place, that any effort on our part to live the Christian life is "of the flesh." We conclude that we should not work at living the Christian life, but simply trust God, who does the work for us. Many of us have tried this approach and, if we are honest with ourselves, have discovered that this, too, is not God's way.

A third way is the "Lord, help me" approach. The chief characteristic of this way is a *partial* dependence on the Lord: the unconscious but nevertheless real attitude that I can of my own self live the Christian life up to a point but that I need the Lord's help *after* that point. It is the assumption—unconscious, perhaps, but still very real—that there is a certain reservoir of goodness, wisdom, and spiritual strength within my own character that I should draw on for the ordinary duties of life, but that beyond that, I need the Lord's help. This may be the attitude of some people who like to quote the saying, "Lord, help me remember that nothing is going to happen to me today that You and I together can't handle." Sadly enough, this is probably the most common approach among sincere Christians today. It is the approach used by thousands of Christians who pray a prayer for God's help at the beginning of the day, but who proceed from that point onward as if it all depended on them—*unless* they meet a crisis situation. It is the attitude most of us fall into at various times if we are not watchful.

But as the great Puritan scholar John Owen wrote, "We do not have the ability in ourselves to accomplish the least of God's tasks. This is a law of grace. When we recognize it is impossible for us to perform a duty in our own strength, we will discover the secret of its accomplishment. But alas, this is a secret we often fail to discover."[9]

The fourth approach to the Christian life is the abiding-in-Christ way. The believer who practices this approach knows that the self-effort approach and the "let go and let God" approach are both futile. He has also learned that he needs God's help not just beyond a certain point but in every aspect of life. He doesn't pray for help just during crises or stressful times. Rather, his prayer is, "Lord, enable me all day long, for without You I can do nothing." To illustrate, let's imagine that God has asked him to lift a heavy log (perhaps the log symbolizes a difficult circumstance he must go through, or just the day-to-day demands of the Christian life). This believer doesn't say, "Lord, I've got a log that's too heavy for me to lift. If You will take one end, I will take the other end and together we will lift this log." Instead he says, "Lord, You must enable me to lift this log if I am to do it. To all appearances it will seem as if I am lifting this log, and I truly am, but I am doing so only because You have given me *all* the strength to do it." This is what Paul was saying in Philippians 4:13: "I can do everything through him who gives me strength." The log in that instance was the challenge of contentment in the midst of changing circumstances. Paul was able to meet that challenge, not with God's help (God and Paul sharing the load) but with God's total enabling.

John Owen again expressed this attitude of total reliance on Christ when he paraphrased Galatians 2:20: "The spiritual life which I have is not my own. I did not induce it, and I cannot maintain it. It is only and solely the work of Christ. It is not I who live, but Christ lives in me. My whole life is His alone."[10]

So the difference between "Lord, help me" and "Lord, enable me" is a matter of partial trust in our self-effort versus total reliance on Christ. When I emphasize this distinction, I am talking about heart attitude, not the words we use. God knows our hearts. If we say or think, "Lord, help me," but our attitude is one of total dependence, God certainly knows what we mean.

The abiding-in-Christ approach ("Lord, enable me") differs greatly from the "let go and let

God" approach in its recognition that as renewed human beings we are called to use all the faculties of our being—our minds, our affections, and our wills—in order to live out the Christian life, but to do so in total dependence on the Holy Spirit working in our minds, our affections, and our wills, empowering us with the power of the risen Christ. "Abiding in Christ" does not denote an absence of conscious effort on our part. Rather, it indicates an all-out effort on our part, but an effort made in total dependence on the Holy Spirit to mediate the life of Christ to us.

Paul gives us a beautiful illustration of this all-out effort made in total dependence on Christ in Colossians 1:28-29: "We proclaim him, admonishing and teaching everyone with all wisdom, so that we may present everyone perfect in Christ. To this end I labor, struggling with all his energy, which so powerfully works in me." In Paul's gospel work he labored, in fact he struggled. "Struggling" in this passage means agonizing. Paul is saying that he labored to the point of agonizing in his effort to present everyone perfect in Christ. There is no doubt that he was conscious of sustained, intense personal effort. Yet he said that he did this "with all [Christ's] energy, which so powerfully works in me." Paul was conscious of personal effort—vigorous effort, in fact—but he was also conscious of his union with Christ, and of the life and power of Christ at work in him.

The awareness that we are in Christ and that through abiding in Him we will "bear much fruit" (John 15:5) should not promote passivity on our part. Rather, it should promote vigorous activity, but activity that is combined with total dependence on Him for the wisdom and strength to carry it through to completion. It is an awareness that all the conscious, visible things we do in the Christian life amount to nothing without His divine enablement. It is an awareness that "unless the LORD builds the house, its builders labor in vain. Unless the LORD watches over the city, the watchmen stand guard in vain" (Psalm 127:1). The person who understands what it means to abide in Christ knows that the builder must work and that the watchmen must guard, but that both must do so in dependence on Jesus Christ.

In this chapter we have looked at fellowship with God as union with Christ. This union is an objective fact, a reality for every Christian, whether we realize it or not. But God intends that we do realize it and that we appropriate the reality of it in our lives through an abiding relationship with Jesus Christ.

In the next chapter we will consider fellowship with God in our daily experience through communion with Him. We need to keep in mind that our *understanding* and *appropriation* of our union with Christ will determine to a large degree the fruitfulness of our communion with Him. I frequently talk to sincere, committed Christians who admit to a dry and mechanical aspect in their quiet times, for example. This is often a result of a subtle dependence on their own discipline rather than a dependence on Christ. We ought to begin our quiet time with the heartfelt prayer, "Lord,

You must enable me to worship You and commune with You today. Without You my mind is dead and my heart is stone."

An understanding and appropriation of our union with Christ will also enhance our fellowship with one another. Fellowship is, after all, not a mere sharing of biblical truth with each other or just having a good social time together. Fellowship is sharing a common life in Christ. Only to the extent that we understand and appropriate the life we have in Christ will we be able to share that life with others.

We will see in later chapters of this book that the full-orbed practice of fellowship involves responsibilities and actions that do not come naturally to us. We cannot rely on our own innate or perhaps culturally induced "goodness" for our practice of koinonia. We must continually abide in Christ, looking to Him for the grace and power to fulfill the responsibilities of true fellowship. But in order to *abide* in Him, we must *know* that we are in Him. Only as we realize in the deepest levels of our understanding that we are branches of the true Vine, Jesus Christ, will we be able to confidently look to Him for all the resources we need to practice fellowship as it is meant to be practiced.

Notes

1. F. W. Grosheide, *The First Epistle to the Corinthians* (Grand Rapids: Eerdmans, 1985), page 32.
2. Matthew Henry, *A Commentary on the Whole Bible* (Old Tappan, NJ: Fleming H. Revell), Volume 6, page 508.

3. Charles Hodge, *An Exposition of the First Epistle to the Corinthians* (London: The Banner of Truth Trust, 1959), pages 10-11.
4. W. E. Vine, *The Epistles of John* (Grand Rapids: Zondervan, 1970), pages 12,14.
5. Donald W. Burdick, *The Epistles of John* (Chicago: Moody Press, 1970), page 21.
6. I. Howard Marshall, *The Epistles of John* (Grand Rapids: Eerdmans, 1978), page 104.
7. Robert Haldane, *Exposition of the Epistle to the Romans* (London: The Banner of Truth Trust, 1958), page 249.
8. This illustration appears on page 80 of the book *Daws*, by Betty Lee Skinner (Grand Rapids: Zondervan, 1974).
9. John Owen, *Sin and Temptation*, abridged and edited by James M. Houston (Portland, OR: Multnomah Press, 1983), page 99.
10. John Owen, page 83.

3
Communion with God

ONE THING I ASK OF THE LORD,
THIS IS WHAT I SEEK:
THAT I MAY DWELL IN THE HOUSE OF THE LORD
ALL THE DAYS OF MY LIFE,
TO GAZE UPON THE BEAUTY OF THE LORD
AND TO SEEK HIM IN HIS TEMPLE.

Psalm 27:4

It was the fall of 1951, and I was a young naval officer serving aboard an amphibious warship in the Far East. The United States was at war with North Korea, and many reservists who had served in the armed forces during World War II had been recalled to active duty during this new conflict. To my knowledge I was the only Christian aboard our ship, which had a complement of some 300 men. I was a fairly new Christian and had quickly discovered that I did not have the spiritual stamina to live the Christian life alone in that rather ungodly atmosphere.

It was in this setting that I was introduced to The Navigators by a fellow naval officer from another ship. We had just returned to the United

States from the Far East, and he invited me to go along with him to a Friday night Bible study at the Navigator home in San Diego. That evening turned out to be the beginning of a life-changing experience for me.

To be perfectly honest, I do not recall anything about the content of the study that evening. I don't remember any of the songs that we sang or anything from the testimonies that were shared. The one thing I do remember as I write these words many years later is the atmosphere. To me, it was almost electric.

It was very obvious that the men attending that Bible study knew God in a personal way that I had never experienced. Most of those men were recalled reservists who had met the Lord or had begun to walk with Him through the ministry of The Navigators during World War II. Even though their lives had now been interrupted by war a second time, they were joyous and victorious in their circumstances because they had a personal relationship with Jesus Christ that sustained them in those circumstances. I soon discovered that "To know Christ and to make Him known" was their motto and that Philippians 3:10, "I want to know Christ . . . ," was one of their key Scripture verses.

Although I knew Christ as my Savior, these men knew Him in a personal, intimate way. They fellowshiped with Him each day through their quiet time, their prayers, their continual meditation on Scriptures they had memorized, and their sharing with others what God had done for them.

To me, Jesus Christ was indeed my Savior, but an impersonal One. He had, according to my understanding, come down from heaven to die for my sins and had returned to heaven. I knew I could pray to Him—and I did sometimes—but there certainly was no sense of a personal relationship with Him on a daily, experiential basis. Even though I knew Christ as Savior and desired to live for Him aboard ship, I knew nothing about a daily relationship with Him that would sustain and nurture that desire.

These men from World War II, a few years older than I, had that personal relationship with Christ, and I wanted what they had. I began to spend as much time as I could around them in order to learn how I too could have such a daily personal relationship with Christ. It was through fellowship with these more mature Christians that I learned to have fellowship with God. But it is important to note that *it was their fellowship with God that attracted me to them and enabled them to teach me how to have fellowship with Him.*

In the previous chapter we saw that the New Testament concept of fellowship with God includes both an objective relationship (union with Christ) and an experiential relationship (communion with Him). We call these two aspects of fellowship with Christ *union* and *communion.* In actuality, however, when we speak of having fellowship with the Lord, we are usually referring to the experiential relationship: our communion with Him.

The semantic distinction between fellowship and communion is not important as long as we understand the reality of both union and communion with Christ. It is the believer's union with Christ, the sharing of His life, that makes possible his communion with Him. When union with Christ is properly understood and embraced, it leads to communion with Him. And communion with Him in turn leads to a greater understanding and appropriation of the blessings of that union. Just as we have looked at the union aspect of fellowship with God, so we must now look at the communion aspect.

An all-day affair

In his little book *Directions for Daily Communion with God,* famed Bible commentator Matthew Henry has written three sections: How to Begin the Day with God, How to Spend the Day with God, and How to Close the Day with God.[1] These three sections point out a very important point regarding communion with God: Our communion should be more than just having a quiet time in the morning; it should be an all-day affair. In fact, Isaiah and David take us one step further. They talk about having communion with the Lord even in the night. Isaiah said, "My soul yearns for you in the night; in the morning my spirit longs for you" (Isaiah 26:9). David said, "On my bed I remember you; I think of you through the watches of the night" (Psalm 63:6).

There is a classic little booklet in circulation written by Brother Lawrence, the cook of a medieval monastery, entitled *The Practice of the Presence of God.* In it Brother Lawrence described how he enjoyed the presence of God as much amid the clatter of his pots and pans in the kitchen as he did in the chapel service each morning.

This is undoubtedly the ideal we should aim for: living continually in the presence of God, whether we are in the classroom, at the office, in the shop, or driving down a busy freeway. Most of us have a problem with this ideal, however. "How," we are inclined to ask, "can I have communion with God when I'm sitting in a university classroom listening to a lecture on economics, or writing a computer program at my job, or checking out groceries in a supermarket? Where am I to find time to think about God and have communion with Him when I have to think about what I'm doing on my job or have to pay attention to what that economics professor is saying? It's all very well for Brother Lawrence to think about God while he washes pots and pans, but I have to use my mind to think about what I'm doing. I can't stop and have communion with God during the day."

These are very legitimate questions, ones for which I have no easy answers, although I will have some suggestions in a few pages. But the real issue is, What is the major thrust of my mind and heart? What do I think about when I do have discretionary thinking time? What do I do when I climb in the car each evening after a busy day? Do I turn on the radio, or do I use that time to have communion with God? I'm not suggesting we should never listen to the car radio. I'm just asking, How do we use our discretionary thinking time? I am personally challenged by the question Dallas Willard asked: "Does our mind spontaneously return to God when not intensely occupied, as the needle of the compass turns to the North Pole when removed from nearer magnetic sources?"[2] If we are serious about communion with God, we must honestly face that question.

The morning quiet time

Just as a house must have a foundation and a framework to hold it together, so our all-day communion with God must have a foundation and a framework to hold it together. The foundation of our communion with God is the morning quiet time.[3]

There is ample evidence, both from Scripture and from the lives of men and women of God of all ages, of the importance of a special time of communing with God the first thing in the morning. David said, "Morning by morning, O LORD, you hear my voice; morning by morning I lay my requests before you and wait in expectation" (Psalm 5:3). It was recorded of Jesus that "very early in the morning, while it was still dark, Jesus got up, left the house and went off to a solitary place where he prayed" (Mark 1:35).

The morning quiet time lays the foundation for our all-day communion with God because it tunes our hearts to commune with Him for the rest of the day. It is a time when we can concentrate all our faculties on worshiping Him in reverent adoration. It is a time when we can give undivided attention to His Word and talk to Him in prayer. It is significant that the Lord Jesus, who was the only one to ever experience unbroken fellowship with the Father, deemed it important to begin His day in prayer. If He felt the need of it, how much more should we!

God calls us to seek His face. Psalm 27:8 says, "When Thou didst say, 'Seek My face,' my heart said to Thee, 'Thy face, O LORD, I shall seek'" (NASB). To the Jewish exiles in Babylonia, God said through Jeremiah, "You will seek me and find me when you seek me with all your heart" (Jeremiah 29:13). There are a dozen or more references in the Bible where we are either encouraged or commanded to seek God's face. The morning quiet time is especially suitable for seeking His face. We may have communion with God throughout the entire day, but seeking His face connotes an intensity of mind and heart that is usually possible only during our time alone with God.

Intense, organized prayer alone with God in the morning prepares us to breathe those quick, silent prayers that are needed so often throughout the day. When Nehemiah heard that the walls of Jerusalem were broken down, he said, "For some days I mourned and fasted and prayed before the God of heaven" (Nehemiah 1:4). God answered his prayers, and one day Nehemiah unexpectantly found himself in a position to make known to the king his desire to return to Jerusalem to rebuild its walls. When King Artaxerxes asked Nehemiah, "What is it you want?" Nehemiah "prayed to the God of heaven, and [then he] answered the king" (Nehemiah 2:4). Nehemiah breathed a quick, silent prayer to God even as he spoke to the king.

But it was those days of praying alone with God that made that quick, silent prayer effective. We all need those quick words of prayer frequently throughout the day, but God will not be satisfied with those alone. All of us have to go to the convenience food store once in a while, but most of us don't do our major grocery shopping there. Likewise, we all need those "quickie" prayers throughout the day, but that is not the time to do major business with God.

Communion throughout the day

Although the morning time with God should lay the foundation for our communion with Him, that communion should not cease at the end of our morning quiet time. Having had time with God in the morning, we are surely not done with Him for the rest of the day. Rather, our entire day is to be spent in devotion to Him, in dependence on Him, in delighting in His fellowship, and in an attitude of doing all that is necessary to please Him.

David, who in Psalm 5:3 said that he waited on God morning by morning, also waited on Him throughout the course of the day. In Psalm 25:5 he said, ". . . for you are God my Savior, and my hope is in you all day long." To hope in God, or to wait on Him, is an expression of expectant dependence on Him. It is the Old Testament equivalent of abiding in Christ. In Chapter 2 we talked about the necessity of abiding in Christ in order to experience His wisdom and power in our lives. This attitude of dependence on Him needs to be so cultivated that it becomes a continuous attitude throughout the day, not just at moments of need as they arise. If it really is true that without Him we can do nothing—and it surely is true—then the habit of depending on Him only at irregularly occurring pressure points during the day leaves much of our lives as a great big zero in God's record book. We need to develop the practice of waiting on God, as David did, *all day long*. Only then will we bear much fruit.

Along with an attitude of waiting on God all day long, we need to learn to walk with Him throughout the day. Enoch found a place in "Faith's Hall of Fame" in Hebrews 11. Yet the Bible only tells us two things about him. He walked with God, and he pleased God (Genesis 5:22,24; Hebrews 11:5). The Dutch commentator G. C. Aalders says, "['Walking with God'] portrays a life lived in spiritual communion with God and which [is] well-pleasing to God."[4]

Matthew Henry says that to walk with God is "to set God always before us, and to act as those that are always under his eye. It is to live a life of communion with God both in ordinances and providences. It is to make God's word our rule and his glory our end in all our actions."[5]

G. C. Aalders and Matthew Henry are saying essentially the same thing. Walking with God signifies a continual communion with Him and a life that is pleasing to Him. The life that is well-pleasing to God results from continual communion with Him. The one flows out of the other.

But there is yet one more reason to enjoy communion with God all day long: to find our delight in Him. David expressed this delight when he said, "Because your love is better than life, my lips will glorify you" (Psalm 63:3). Paul expressed it in those famous words, "To me, to live is Christ . . ." (Philippians 1:21). I believe the ultimate purpose of continual communion with God is simply to enjoy Him. Because godly Samuel Rutherford found this delight in Him, he could write from his bleak prison cell, "One smile of Christ's face is now to me as a kingdom."

Most of us do not experience this continual communion and corresponding delight in God that the Bible talks about. Worse yet, we do not even long for it. We are content to *use* God—to seek His help in our jobs, our studies, our marriages, and, yes, even our ministries. Since these are all legitimate needs, we surely do need God's help in all of them. But God is pleased when we find our delight *in Him alone.* And to those who sincerely delight in *Him*, not just in His blessings, He promises, "Delight yourself in the LORD and he will give you the desires of your heart" (Psalm 37:4). Our prayer ought to be that God will enable us to so commune with Him throughout the day that we will truly find our delight in Him.

How do we then practice communion with God throughout the day? If the morning quiet time is the foundation of that communion, Scripture meditation and prayer are the framework of it. Meditation on the Word of God both "day and night" is both commanded and commended (Joshua 1:8, Psalm 1:2). And we are to "pray continually" (1 Thessalonians 5:17). Few Christians take these instructions seriously. We have tacitly written them off as impractical in today's busy world.

But it can be done. It takes serious commitment and mental discipline, but we can practice communion with God throughout the day. It begins with Scripture memorization. We can meditate on Scripture—think about it and reflect on it—throughout the day only if we have it in our minds. And we have Scripture in our minds only if we have made the effort to just plain memorize it. There is no shortcut to meditation that bypasses Scripture memorization.

Dawson Trotman, founder of The Navigators, was used by God to help the twentieth-century evangelical Church recover the scriptural emphasis of discipleship. Today discipleship is a common concept and well-used term in many Christian organizations and hundreds of churches. To Dawson Trotman, Scripture memorization was absolutely essential to discipleship; yet few churches and organizations seriously promote it. I wonder: Can we truly have discipleship without a serious emphasis on Scripture memorization? I doubt it.

But assuming we have begun to memorize Scripture, how then do we use it to have communion with God? We need to develop the habit throughout the day of continually turning our minds to the Word of God, reflecting on it *each time opportunity permits*. This means that every time we *can* choose what we will think about, we choose to think about the Word of God. But we don't just think about the bare words of Scripture. We think beyond the words to the God of Scripture, for we realize that through the words of those Scriptures God is speaking to us. As we listen to Him speak through this meditation, we can then speak back to Him, acknowledging what He is saying to us and, as appropriate, thanking Him, praising Him, responding to His will, or perhaps confessing our failures to respond to His will. Whatever response to a particular Scripture is appropriate for us at a given time should become the subject of immediate prayer along with our meditation.

To "pray continually," however, should not be understood only in terms of our responses to Scripture meditation. As we go through the day and find those discretionary thinking times, there will be other subjects we will want to bring to God in prayer. There are friends and loved ones who have needs, and there is a continual need for guidance, wisdom, and strength for ourselves. There are certain problems and situations we face that can be resolved only by God. All of these matters are valid subjects for our communion with God throughout the course of the day. But with all of this, let us not just "conduct business" with God. Let us take time to simply enjoy Him and let Him enjoy us. Any relationship, whether it is a marriage, a friendship, or even a supervisor-employee relationship, soon deteriorates if it is simply built on "conducting business."

People must truly like one another and enjoy one another if they are to establish and maintain solid relationships. So it is in our relationship with God. We must get beyond merely "conducting business" with God and further establish the reality of the Father-child relationship we already have with Him.

But the Scriptures portray another relationship with God that is even more intimate than that suggested by the Father-child bond. The Father-child relationship suggests to us such concepts as dependency and care, need and provision. But the Scriptures also set forth a relationship between God and His people of love, intimacy, and sweet communion. This relationship is that of Christ and His Church, the Bridegroom and His Bride. And while the Bride of Christ is the entire Body of believers, the individual Christian has the privilege of enjoying that intimate relationship with Christ as if he or she were the sole object of His affections.

Many Bible commentators agree that the little-known Bible book known as the Song of Songs, or as it is more commonly called, the Song of Solomon, depicts the love and communion between Christ and His Church. It is a book rich in terms of endearment, affection, and tenderness between the Lover (Christ) and His Beloved (the Church).

For example, the Lover says, "How beautiful you are, my darling! Oh, how beautiful! Your eyes are doves" (Song of Songs 1:15). In 2:2 the Lover says, "Like a lily among thorns is my darling among the maidens." To this the Beloved replies, "Like an apple tree among the trees of the forest is my lover among the young men. I delight to sit in his shade, and his fruit is sweet to my taste. He has taken me to the banquet hall, and his banner over me is love" (2:3-4).

These words of affection and love are intended to portray the love between Christ and His Church—the expression of intimate communion we have with Him. Yet how many Christians ever profit from meditating on the Song of Songs? Is it not because there are so few of us who can identify to any degree with the love relationship and intimate communion between Christ and His people that is depicted in that little book?

Our emphasis today is on doing things for God, or on believing the right doctrines about God. But few believers take time to commune with God simply for the sake of enjoying Him and adoring Him. In the Church today there seems to be very little of that thirst for God described by the psalmist who said, "As the deer pants for streams of water, so my soul pants for you, O God" (Psalm 42:1).

Some have even suggested that such intimate communion with Christ is reserved for only a select few: the so-called mystics within the Church of Jesus Christ. But if all Scripture is indeed profitable for all believers, then the examples of Enoch and Abraham, of Moses and David, and of the Apostles John and Paul, all men who experienced intimate communion with God, are given to *all* of us to follow. I well remember a number of years ago thinking about Paul's intense desire to know Christ, to experience a deeper and more intimate communion with Him. As I thought over that verse, Philippians 3:10, I said, "Lord, I cannot identify with Paul's desire, but I would like to." Over the years God has gradually answered that prayer. I am certainly no mystic, but I do thank God for the privilege of personal communion with Him throughout the course of my day.

In his classic book *The Pursuit of God*, A. W. Tozer quotes a verse from the well-known hymn "Jesus, Thou Joy of Loving Hearts" that sets forth so beautifully the emotion that should well up in the heart of every believer every day:

> We taste Thee, O Thou living bread,
> And long to feast upon Thee still;
> We drink of Thee, the Fountainhead,
> And thirst our souls from Thee to fill.

It was this desire for intimate communion with Christ that set apart those World War II navy men I met in San Diego. They were common, ordinary men fulfilling common, ordinary duties every day aboard their ships and stations. But they longed to know Christ more intimately, and their longing was contagious. They passed it on to me.

Sharing with God

There is yet one further aspect of communion with God that we must consider. In Chapter 1, we saw that one of the meanings of koinonia is to share what we have with one another, whether what we share is spiritual truth or material possessions. We call the sharing of spiritual truth *communion*; we often refer to this as fellowship.

As we think of communion with God, one question that might arise as a result of our definition is, What can *I* share with God? We readily see what God can share with us. We think of such things as enlightenment from His Word, answers to prayer, peace in the midst of anxious circumstances, and power to live a godly life and to witness to others. But what can I share with God? Is communion with Him a one-way street in which He shares His blessings with me and I only receive them?

One of the amazing privileges that believers have is to share with God in communion, actually giving something to Him. God is entirely self-sufficient and complete in Himself. Although He needs nothing from us, He has given us the privilege of sharing with Him. Revelation 4:6-9 speaks of four living creatures around God's throne who give glory, honor, and thanks to Him. This provides us one clue as to what we can give to God. We can give worship and thanksgiving, worshiping Him for who He is and thanking Him for all He has done for us. David's prayer of worship and thanksgiving recorded in 1 Chronicles 29:10-14 and the songs of worship recorded in Revelation 4:11, 5:9-10, and 5:12-13 are models for us of sharing with God.

Something else that we can give to God is our love through our obedience. Jesus said that those who obey Him are the ones who truly love Him. Now obedience is carried out in the course of daily living, but it is in our time of communion with God that we see His moral will for us. It is at that time that we set our wills to obey Him. The Bible indicates that God is pleased when our hearts are humbled before His Word and responsive to its commands. We give to God when we respond to His Word with a commitment of loving obedience.

Even our confessions of sin can be a time of sharing with God if we have the right attitude. If our confessions are God-centered rather than self-centered, they can be a time of worship. Two excellent examples of worship in the midst of confession are found in Ezra 9:5-15 and Nehemiah 9:5-35. Both of these prayers acknowledge not only the sins of the Jews but also the righteousness, justice, and graciousness of God in His dealings with them. Verses such as these—"You have punished us less than our sins have deserved" (Ezra 9:13), and "In all that has happened to us, you have been just; you have acted faithfully, while we did wrong" (Nehemiah 9:33)—are expressions of worship in the midst of confession.

All too often, however, our prayers of confession are self-centered. We are not so much interested in giving glory to God as we are in getting rid of our own sense of guilt. We lightly acknowledge our sins, boldly rather than humbly claiming the forgiveness and cleansing promised in 1 John 1:9. We fail to deal with the fundamental fact that we have not only been impatient with someone, for example, but that we have also sinned against an infinitely holy God. But if we decide to make our times of confession God-centered, then we can turn even confession into an expression of worship to Him.

As we give to God, He in turn gives to us. In fact, His giving precedes ours, for it is through the ministry of His Spirit in our hearts that we are prompted to give Him worship, thanksgiving, and obedience. God gives us a sense of His presence, and through that a fullness of joy. He enlightens our minds to understand the Scriptures so that we say along with the Emmaus-road disciples, "Were not our hearts burning within us while he talked with us on the road and opened the Scriptures to us?" (Luke 24:32). He calms our anxieties and assures us of His faithfulness through the precious promises in His Word. He gives us the privilege of entering the sanctuary of His own heart, and there we gain a burden for the sin and misery of this world that so grieves our Lord. These and many more expressions of His love await the person who will take time to seriously enter into communion with God.

The Bible indicates from its earliest chapters that God prizes our communion. In Genesis 3, we find God walking in the garden, calling out for Adam so that He might have fellowship with him. We read in Genesis 5 of Enoch walking, or communing, with God. We learn of God speaking with Moses face to face, as a man speaks with his friend. We hear David's intense desire for communion with God as he cries out, "O God, you are my God, earnestly I seek you; my soul thirsts for you, my body longs for you, in a dry and weary land where there is no water" (Psalm 63:1).

Turning to the New Testament, we read Jesus' promise to the one who obeys Him that He and the Father "will come to him and make our home with him" (John 14:23), which is communion between God and man. We see Paul's intense desire to know Christ better in Philippians 3:10, and read of Jesus' knocking at our heart's door so that He may come in and eat with us, symbolic of His strong desire to fellowship with us. What a glorious truth that the infinite and eternal God in the Persons of both the Father and the Son desires to have fellowship with us through the Holy Spirit. God has called us into the fellowship of His Son Jesus Christ. He has called us into a living relationship with Him by placing us *in Christ*, and He has called us to experience the joy and power of that relationship by having daily communion with Him.

This vertical aspect of fellowship (union and communion with God) provides both the foundation and the pattern for the horizontal aspect (fellowship among believers). A community relationship among believers presupposes a living relationship with God and is, in fact, dependent on it. Where there is no vital union with Christ, there can be no sharing of the common life that believers have in Him. In the same manner, if believers are to share with one another in communion, they must first have something to share, something obtained only through communion with God. As we now turn our attention to the horizontal aspects of fellowship—the sharing of the common life and the sharing with one another that flows out of that life—let us keep in mind that it is all made possible by our vertical fellowship with God.

Notes

1. Matthew Henry, *Directions For Daily Communion With God* (Grand Rapids: Baker Book House, 1978).
2. Dallas Willard, *In Search of Guidance* (Ventura, CA: Regal Books, 1984), page 177.
3. I assume that most readers are familiar with the morning quiet time and do not need instruction in the "how to" of that practice. For those who do want some practical guidance, I recommend *Quiet Time,* published by InterVarsity Press, and *Seven Minutes With God,* published by NavPress.
4. G. Charles Aalders, *Bible Student's Commentary: Genesis,* Volume 1 (Grand Rapids: Zondervan, 1981), page 141.
5. Matthew Henry, *A Commentary of the Whole Bible,* Volume 1, page 49.

4
Fellowship Is a Community

IN CHRIST WE WHO ARE MANY
FORM ONE BODY, AND EACH
MEMBER BELONGS TO ALL
THE OTHERS.

Romans 12:5

God does not save groups; He saves individual people. Each of us must respond individually in repentance and faith to the gospel invitation. But though God saves us as individuals, He immediately incorporates us into the Body of Christ. As Paul said in 1 Corinthians 12:13, "We were all baptized by one Spirit into one body—whether Jews or Greeks, slaves or free." Every believer of every nation, race, or station in life is a member of that Body. From all over the world, God has drawn together a spiritual community whose members share a common life in Christ. Koinonia expresses, first of all, the relationship that the members of this Christ-centered community have with God and with each other.

The community aspect of fellowship does not refer to a geographical location. Neither does it refer to a group of believers who have chosen to live in a close physical setting to accomplish certain spiritual and physical objectives. Though such groups may rightfully call themselves a "community," this is not the sense in which we use the word to describe the communal sense of koinonia. Rather, koinonia expresses a relationship all believers have together in Christ without regard to their geographical location.

It is also true that koinonia expresses more than membership in a local congregation. We sometimes refer to "extending the right hand of fellowship" when we welcome new members into our various churches. As important as membership in a local congregation is, koinonia expresses even more than that. The relationship expressed by koinonia does not describe a membership but a common life that we share together in Christ. When Paul uses the metaphor of a human body to describe the family of God, he uses it to express the spiritually organic relationship that we have with Christ and with all fellow believers all over the world.

An objective fact

All believers share a common life in Christ, whether or not we recognize it. We are in fellowship with literally thousands of believers from every nation of the world. Although we have never met most of them, yet we are in fellowship with them. We disagree with many of them over various issues of faith and practice, yet we are still members of the same Body. Even though we struggle to like some of them, that does not alter the fact that we share together a common life in Christ. Neither our attitudes nor our actions affect this objective sense of koinonia. We are in fellowship with all other believers, whether or not we like it or even recognize the fact.

This objective truth of koinonia is meant to provide the foundation for the experiential aspects of fellowship. The realization that we do in fact share a common life with other believers should stimulate within us a desire to share experientially with one another. This is the whole thrust of the New Testament teaching on koinonia.

To be objectively in fellowship with other believers while we experientially deny that very fellowship is to contradict the clear teaching of the Bible and to live in disobedience to the revealed will of God. Paul tells us in Romans 12:5 that "each member [of the Body] belongs to all the others." There is a mutual ownership of one another: I belong to you and you belong to me, and we each belong to all the other members of the Body. This is an objective statement of fact. But because we *do* belong to one another, we are to express this belonging in acts of mutual concern and caring for one another.

Just after telling us that we belong to one another, Paul applies this truth in some very practical admonitions: "Be devoted to one another . . . honor one another . . . share with God's people who are in need . . . rejoice with those who rejoice;

mourn with those who mourn" (Romans 12:10, 13,15). This is experiential fellowship, the biblical practice of koinonia. But it can only occur when the members of the Body recognize that they are in objective fellowship—that they do share a common life in Christ with one another.

Caring for one another

The truth that we belong to one another should work itself out in our lives in a number of mutually helpful ways. Paul says that all the parts of the Body "should have equal concern for each other" (1 Corinthians 12:25). What is our response, for example, when we hear of a fellow believer who has fallen before some temptation? Is it a response of criticism and condemnation, of gossip and a holier-than-thou shaking of our heads? If so, we are not practicing biblical koinonia. Instead of criticism and condemnation, there should be concern and prayer for our fellow member of the Body and, if it is appropriate, attempts on our part to gently restore the erring brother or sister.

Let me illustrate the utter ridiculousness of some of our attitudes and actions toward other believers with a somewhat silly idea. Can you imagine the ear making the following comment to the eye? "Say, did you hear about the serious trouble the foot is having? My, my, isn't it too bad? That foot surely ought to get his act together." No, no, our bodies don't behave that way at all! Instead the entire body cries out, "My foot hurts! I feel awful!"

Why does the whole body hurt when only one

part is injured? It is because all the parts of the body make up one indivisible whole. And when one part hurts, no matter what the reason, the restorative powers of the entire body are brought to bear on that hurting member. Rather than attacking that suffering part or ignoring the problem, the rest of the body demonstrates concern for the part that hurts. This is the way the Body of Christ should function.

So often we find ourselves saying something like, "Say, did you hear about Harry and Sue? It seems they're really having some problems. They're even thinking about a divorce. It's too bad. Why can't people get along with each other anymore?" Just as the parts of the physical body never communicate with such negativity and indifference, neither should we. Rather, we should rush the restorative powers of the Body to those hurting members. Basically this means that the ministry of the Holy Spirit needs to be applied by the loving and concerned prayer of other members. Even in this area, though, we need to be careful that we do not gossip under the guise of sharing a prayer request. Every word we say about the hurting of another believer should be motivated strictly by a sincere concern for that person's welfare and a desire to see the restorative power of the Holy Spirit at work in his or her life.

One of the real scandals of the Church is the way believers so often slander one another with gossip and criticism. We have divided sins into acceptable and unacceptable categories. We condemn sexual immorality while we tolerate slander in the Body. Paul says, however, that neither the sexually immoral nor slanderers shall inherit the Kingdom of God (1 Corinthians 6:9-10). The solution to this scandalous activity in the Body is a keener awareness of the biblical meaning of fellowship. Only as we become acutely aware of the truth that we *are* in fellowship with every other believer—like it or not—will we seek to work out the implications of that fellowship in loving concern and care for each other.

Honoring one another

Not only should our fellowship be characterized by concern and care instead of condemnation and criticism; we should go even a step further. Paul tells us to "honor one another above yourselves" (Romans 12:10). Just as the practice of true fellowship tends to eliminate condemnation and criticism, so it should also tend to eliminate *competition* among believers. When another part of the Body is honored, we should rejoice because that part of the Body belongs to us and we belong to it. Here again we characteristically fall woefully short of the biblical ideal because we do not recognize the objective nature of biblical fellowship. We tend to think of ourselves individually or as members of a particular group of Christians rather than as members of the Body of Christ.

When we think individualistically rather than corporately, we foster competition rather than cooperation and honor. Moses is a good example of the spirit of cooperation and honor. On one occasion during the Israelites' journey in the wilderness, God took the Spirit He had given Moses and put Him on seventy of the elders who were with Moses at the Tent of Meeting. When the Spirit rested on them they began to prophesy, that is, they began to speak the word of the Lord as did Moses. Two of the elders, however, had remained in the camp. They had failed for some reason to go out to be with Moses. Yet the Spirit rested on them and they, too, began to prophesy.

Joshua, who was Moses' aide at the time, wanted Moses to stop the two elders back in the camp. After all, they were not part of the group, at least at that particular moment; they were not at the tent with the other elders supporting Moses. Joshua was jealous for Moses' authority; he didn't like the idea of someone not closely involved with Moses sharing that authority. But Moses was not concerned. In a classic statement of humility and largeness of heart, Moses replied to Joshua, "Are you jealous for my sake? I wish that all the LORD's people were prophets and that the LORD would put his Spirit on them!" (Numbers 11:29). Moses was not concerned for his own authority; he was concerned for the people of God. He was thinking corporately rather than competitively.

How do we respond when God blesses some other individual or another church or another Christian organization? Are we jealous for our own sake, or even for the sake of our church, or for our particular Christian group? How should the Christian student on campus react when God seems to bless another Christian campus organization more than the one in which he is involved? If that student has a concept of biblical fellowship, he will recognize that we all belong to one another and he will rejoice in the fact that God is blessing the Body, even though it is a different part of the Body than the part he is involved in. To the extent that he recognizes Christian fellowship as primarily a community of all believers in Christ, he will be able to respond to Paul's admonition to "honor one another above yourselves." In fact, the recognition that true fellowship reflects a sense of community among all believers goes a long way toward resolving any number of interpersonal, interchurch (as well as intra-church), and interorganizational problems. It is difficult to be critical or jealous of someone who belongs to you.

Reproving one another

Such a concept of community does not require us to compromise our convictions, but it does require us to express them in a loving and caring manner. We may be concerned for the purity of the Church or for the testimony of Christ on our campus. But we must also be concerned for those members of the Body whose actions are causing us concern. If they are true believers, they, too, are God's special people just as we are. God will not reject them and neither should we. He may admonish and discipline them, but He does so out of a spirit of love, not of rejection. Even to that proud and lukewarm church at Laodicea, God said, "Those whom I love I rebuke and discipline" (Revelation 3:19). Amazingly enough, He invited those proud, lukewarm people to repent and open their hearts to

Him so that He could come in and have fellowship with them! Instead of rejection, God offered loving rebuke and an appeal for fellowship.

God did not compromise His standards with the Christians at Laodicea. He rebuked them and called for repentance, and yet He did it in a loving, caring manner. Instead of rejecting them, He sought a restoration of fellowship. Even though they were the offending party, He took the initiative. He did so because those proud, lukewarm believers at Laodicea belonged to Him.

It is just as true today that believers who offend us by their words and actions, and who we may feel are a reproach to the name of Christ, still belong to God. And because they belong to Him, they belong to us as well. If God does not reject them but instead seeks their restoration, then we should do the same.

Praying for one another

An understanding of biblical fellowship as a community of believers will deeply affect our prayer lives. For many years I took an individualistic approach to the Christian life. I was concerned about *my* growth as a Christian, *my* progress in holiness, *my* acquisition of ministry skills. I prayed that God would enable *me* to be more holy in my personal life and more effective in my evangelism. I asked for God's blessing on *my* church and the Christian organization *I* worked for. But as I learned more about true fellowship, I began to pray that *we* as the Body of Christ would grow in holiness, that *we* would be more effective witnesses to the saving grace of Christ. It is the entire Body—not just me—that needs to grow.

Of course we cannot ignore our individual, personal responsibility to grow in the Christian life. The Body grows as each member grows. But the ultimate focus of our concern should be the same as God's: growth of the whole Body. I should be as concerned about the other members' growth as I am about my own growth. There is no room for self-absorbed individualism in the New Testament concept of fellowship. There has to be, of course, recognition of personal responsibility by every believer to grow and fulfill his or her function in the Body. This is decidedly different, however, from an individualistic attitude focusing primarily on one's own growth, or the growth of one's own group, to the exclusion of the interests of the Body as a whole.

Today there is a renewed emphasis on discipleship of the individual. This is good and healthy because the Body can only grow as its individual members grow. Amid his concern for all the churches, Paul could say, "You know that we dealt with *each of you* as a father deals with his own children" (1 Thessalonians 2:11, italics added). Paul discipled individuals, but he related them to the Body because at their salvation they had become members of the Body.

In Ephesians 4:16 Paul struck a beautiful balance between his concern for the individual and his concern for the Body. He said, "From [Christ] the whole body, joined and held together by every supporting ligament, grows and builds itself up in love, as each part does its work." Paul recognized that the Body does not grow unless each member grows and does his work. He was concerned for the individual believer. But he also recognized that the larger purpose of each member's growing and working is the building up of the entire Body in love. God is uniquely concerned for each individual, but He is ultimately concerned about the Body. As we recognize that biblical fellowship is, first of all, a community relationship of all believers, then we, too, will be concerned about the growth and health of Christ's Body.

5
Spiritual Fellowship

ENCOURAGE ONE ANOTHER DAILY, AS LONG AS IT IS CALLED TODAY, SO THAT NONE OF YOU MAY BE HARDENED BY SIN'S DECEITFULNESS.

Hebrews 3:13

One day I received an urgent phone call from a Christian friend asking if we could have lunch together that day. We get together periodically over lunch or breakfast to share what God is doing in our lives, to encourage and counsel one another, and to share prayer requests. I'm not discipling him, nor is he discipling me. We're both involved in ministering to others, but we need and appreciate the mutual strengthening that comes from these times together.

That day, however, wasn't just an ordinary time together. My friend was hurting. Over lunch he poured out his heart to me concerning some difficult problems he was facing at work. I listened, offered a suggestion or two from the Scriptures as to how he should respond, and committed myself to pray for him. As I drove back to my office I did pray for him, and when I arrived home that evening I jotted down his need on my "emergency" prayer list.

His situation did not improve suddenly and dramatically, but over a period of several months God did answer our prayers. During that time I continued to encourage him, to pray for him, and to explore various alternatives with him until we saw God work.

This incident illustrates the importance and vital necessity of *spiritual fellowship,* or what I called in Chapter 1 "communion" with one another.[1] God has created us to be dependent both on Him and on one another. His judgment that "it is not good for the man to be alone" (Genesis 2:18) is a principle that speaks not only to the marriage relationship but also to the necessity of spiritual fellowship among all believers. None of us has the spiritual wherewithal to "go it alone" in our Christian lives.

Spiritual fellowship is not a luxury but a necessity, vital to our spiritual growth and health. We have seen that biblical fellowship involves both a sharing together of our common life in Christ and a sharing with one another what God has given to us. One of the most important things we can share with one another is the spiritual truth that God has been teaching us, which might be of great help to fellow believers.

J. I. Packer has an interesting insight about this type of fellowship:

> We should not . . . think of our fellowship with other Christians as a spiritual luxury, an optional addition to the exercises of private devotion. We should recognize rather that such fellowship is a spiritual necessity; for God has made us in such a way that our fellowship with himself is fed by our fellowship with fellow-Christians, and requires to be so fed constantly for its own deepening and enrichment.[2]

Scripture contains a number of exhortations and examples on this subject. For example, Solomon says in Proverbs 27:17, "As iron sharpens iron, so one man sharpens another." It is in the exchange with each other of that which God is teaching us that our minds and hearts are whetted and stimulated. We learn from one another as together we learn from God.

Solomon, writing in Ecclesiastes, said, "Two are better than one, because they have a good return for their work: If one falls down, his friend can help him up. But pity the man who falls and has no one to help him up!" (Ecclesiastes 4:9-10).

Solomon intended more than simply a literal application of these truths to physical situations. In his rather picturesque way, he was emphasizing the importance of fellowship. Two are better than one, first, because of the synergistic effect: Two together can produce more than each of them working alone. Two Christians sharing the Word together can learn more than the two of them studying individually. They stimulate one another. Second, two people together can help each other up when they fall or even when they are in danger of falling. One of the many advantages of fellowship is the mutual admonishing or encouraging of one another in the face of a temptation or an attack of Satan.

The writer of Hebrews was rather emphatic about the importance of this aspect of fellowship. In Hebrews 3:13 he said, "Encourage one another daily, as long as it is called Today, so that none of you may be hardened by sin's deceitfulness." Then in Hebrews 10:24-25 he said, "Let us consider how we may spur one another on toward love and good deeds. Let us not give up meeting together, as some are in the habit of doing, but let us encourage one another—and all the more as you see the Day approaching." Note the emphasis on encouraging one another in the face of temptation and spurring one another on toward love and good deeds. We need to be kept from temptation and we need to be stimulated when our zeal for Christian duty is flagging.

The admonition of Hebrews 10:24-25—"Let us not give up meeting together"—is not fulfilled merely by attending church on Sunday morning, as is so often supposed. Rather, it is fulfilled only when we follow through with the instruction to encourage, spur on, or stimulate one another. This cannot be done sitting in pews, row upon row, listening to the pastor teach. It can only be done through the mutual interchange of admonishment and encouragement. This is not to diminish the importance of the teaching ministry of our pastors. The Bible makes it quite clear that their ministry holds a vital place in our lives (see, for example, Ephesians 4:11-12, 1 Thessalonians 4:1, 1 Timothy 3:2, 1 Timothy 5:17, 2 Timothy 4:2). But we need both the public teaching of our pastors and the mutual encouragement and admonishing of one another. It is this latter that seems to be the main thrust of Hebrews 10:24-25.

I have earlier referred to fellowship as one of the four "spokes" of the Navigator Wheel illustration. It has not always been one of the spokes, but was added at a later date because of the recognition of the vital importance of mutual encouragement and admonishment of others in maintaining our relationship with the Lord.

We also need this type of fellowship in order to keep us laboring in our respective areas of ministry. Because Jesus emphasized that "the harvest is plentiful but the workers are few" (Matthew 9:37), The Navigators have made it their aim to train dedicated laborers for the harvest fields of the world. But what is it that keeps a person laboring once he has "graduated" from our training environment and is out on his own in the community? Although a number of things are important, high on the list is this type of fellowship: the encouragement and accountability of another person of like mind. The demands of family and job and other legitimate responsibilities may distract us from the ministry to which God has called us unless we are encouraged and spurred on by other believers who share our vision.

Even the Apostle Paul, spiritual giant that he was, recognized his need for fellowship with other believers. Writing to the church in Rome, he expressed the desire "that you and I may be mutually encouraged by each other's faith" (Romans 1:12). He wanted to strengthen the faith of the Roman Christians, but he also wanted them to strengthen his. He constantly acknowledged his need for other believers.

Historically, the Church's Apostles' Creed speaks of "the communion of saints," referring no doubt to both the objective community relationship and the experiential sharing of spiritual fellowship with one another. Packer tells us, "The Puritans used to ask God for one 'bosom friend,' with whom they could share absolutely everything and maintain a full-scale prayer-partner relationship; and with that they craved, and regularly set up, group conversations about divine things."[3]

We see, then, that the Bible teaches us the importance of spiritual fellowship and that Church history affirms it. But how do we go about it? How can we have the kind of spiritual fellowship the Bible talks about?

First, spiritual fellowship with one another presupposes fellowship with God. If we are not having communion with God and learning from Him, we will have nothing to share with others. In addition, if we are not learning directly from God, we will not be alert and perceptive enough to learn from others. We will be dull of hearing.

Packer says, "Fellowship with God, then, is the source from which fellowship among Christians springs; and fellowship with God is the end to which Christian fellowship is a means."[4] Fellowship with God is indeed both the foundation and the objective of our fellowship with one another.

Second, spiritual fellowship involves mutual commitment and responsibility. We must commit ourselves to faithfulness in getting together, openness and honesty with one another, and confidentiality in what is shared. We must assume the responsibility to encourage, admonish, and pray for one another. Spiritual fellowship means that we "watch out" for one another, feeling a mutual responsibility for each other's welfare. This does not mean that we transfer the responsibility for our Christian walk to another person or that we assume his, but rather that we help each other through encouragement and accountability.

Such a high level of commitment is normally made with just one person or a few selected people. Such a depth of fellowship simply cannot be maintained with every Christian, nor does God intend it. Though objectively we are in fellowship with every other believer throughout the world, in our subjective personal experience such fellowship can be maintained with only a few. We must look to God to lead us to the few special people with whom we can develop such a commitment and sense of responsibility.

As we accept the fact that spiritual fellowship with one another implies a personal fellowship with God and a mutual commitment to one another, we can then look at some practical suggestions, some specific activities that will help us experience vital fellowship with one another.

Sharing biblical truth

First, we must share the dynamic truth of Scripture with one another. Spiritual fellowship should always be centered around the teaching of the Bible. The Apostle John made the truth concerning Jesus Christ the basis of his call to fellowship (1 John 1:1-3). I have already mentioned the synergistic effect that occurs when two or more believers share together what God is teaching them.

The psalmist said to God, "With my lips I recount all the laws that come from your mouth" (Psalm 119:13). He declared to others what God was teaching him. Through this exercise, he not only edified others but also strengthened his own understanding of God's truth. There is an old adage that says, "Words disentangle themselves when passing over the lips or through the pencil tips." As we share our thoughts with others, we learn because we are forced to organize and develop our ideas.

Some Christians feel threatened by this kind of fellowship. They feel that they have nothing to share. They are terrified by the question, "What has God been teaching you recently?" A practical way to overcome this fear of sharing is to record daily the most important truth you get from your Bible-reading that day. You may want to write a sentence or a paragraph, depending on the fullness of your thinking on that particular truth. Then arrange to get together weekly with an understanding Christian friend—perhaps someone who shares your fear of sharing openly—and pass on to each other what you have learned from the Scriptures that week.

Another way to begin to share with someone is to memorize Scripture together. That is, although you must work on memorizing the verses as individuals, you can get together once a week to quote your verses to each other and share what God has taught you from those verses. As you do this on a regular basis, you will experience the iron-sharpening-iron effect described in Proverbs 27:17.

Whether it comes from reading, study, or memorization of the Bible, the sharing of biblical truth with one another should be done in a way that makes it relevant to your daily life. It is not enough to tell someone what fresh insight you have gained from the Scriptures. What do those insights mean to you in a practical way? How have you grown through them? How have you applied them or how do you plan to apply them? It is the *application* of Scripture, not just the academic knowledge of it, that makes it fruitful in our lives.

Those who have learned to share easily with others what they are learning from God face the danger of failing to listen to what another Christian is saying. Too often we are so eager to share what we have learned that we fail to hear what God is saying to us through another believer. In such a case, we are not really interested in fellowship but in displaying our own knowledge of Scripture. We are playing spiritual one-upmanship. For those who have this temptation, it would be well to remember the words of Jesus when He prayed, "I praise you, Father . . . because you have hidden these things from the wise and learned, and revealed them to little children" (Luke 10:21). God may very well have something to say to us through one who speaks with stammering lips and a halting tongue.

Openness with one another

Spiritual fellowship, however, involves more than the mutual sharing of scriptural truths. It also involves the sharing of our sins, failures, and discouragements, as well as our blessings and joys. And throughout all our spiritual fellowship we need to have a view to mutual exhortation, encouragement, and prayer. James told us, "Confess your sins to each other and pray for each other so that you may be healed" (James 5:16).

This aspect of fellowship is threatening to most of us. We hesitate to expose our sins, or even our doubts and discouragements. Our problem, of course, is pride—the fear of what another person will think of us if he knows how we have sinned. We forget that "no temptation has seized [us] except what is common to man" (1 Corinthians 10:13). Very likely the friend with whom you are seeking to have fellowship is struggling with the same temptation, or at least with another one that he or she is equally embarrassed about.

We cannot encourage, motivate, or pray for one another if we do not know the struggles the other person is facing. Remember Packer's statement about the Puritans? They asked God for a friend with whom they could share absolutely everything. We need to ask God for such a close friend. And then, after we find that friend, we need to be willing to open our lives to him or her.

Accountability

Spiritual fellowship involves more than openness with one another; it also calls for mutual accountability. The ideas of admonishing one another (Colossians 3:16) and submitting to one another (Ephesians 5:21) both suggest the concept of mutual accountability. Accountability is the willingness to be both checked on and challenged in agreed-on areas of one's life. For example, if you and I have committed ourselves to spiritual fellowship, we might agree to be accountable to each other in certain disciplines: a regular quiet time, Bible study, Scripture memorization, and meditation. As we meet together regularly, we give account to one another regarding our progress in those areas.

Another area of accountability is the area of so-called weaknesses. These weaknesses may be due to frailties of the temperament (such as lack of discipline in time management or lack of self-control), or they may be due to "besetting sins," those temptations to which we are particularly vulnerable. If you are struggling with a temperament weakness or a particularly compelling temptation, you need to be willing to share those problems with someone you are close to in the Lord. Asking for that person's prayer support and voluntarily becoming accountable to him will provide you with great strength in overcoming that weakness or resisting that temptation.

Accountability is especially important in a discipleship training context and in a one-to-one relationship. This book does not focus on discipleship training as such, but the concept of spiritual fellowship must be an integral part of any one-to-one building in another's life. Successful teaching and training cannot occur on such a close personal level unless there is a mutual trust, openness, concern, and accountability. The person being discipled must be accountable to the discipler; otherwise the whole discipling process is futile. But the discipler must also be willing to open his life to the other person in order to build rapport and gain confidence. My own experience has been that as I am open about my own failures and weaknesses with the person I am discipling, he is encouraged to be open with me.

Praying together

The fourth ingredient of fellowship is praying with and for one another. The Puritans not only wanted someone with whom they could share absolutely everything, but they also wanted a person with whom they could maintain a full-scale prayer-partner relationship.

Oftentimes we have prayer needs that are not appropriate for sharing in our local congregations or campus ministry groups, or even in our small group Bible studies. But we can share these needs with our "bosom friend." No prayer request should seem so insignificant or embarrassing that we would not feel free to mention it to the friend with whom we have intimate spiritual fellowship.

I have already mentioned the twofold concept of commitment and responsibility. If I have made a mutual commitment with and assumed a spiritual responsibility for someone else, that responsibility cannot be fulfilled without the mutual dedication to prayer. God works in another person's life largely as a result of prayer. He may use my sharing from the Scriptures and my words of admonishment and encouragement, but He does so as a result of my prayers. My own study of the Scriptures, verified by personal experience, has convinced me that prayer is the most important ministry I can have in the life of another individual. So if I truly want to have a close spiritual relationship with another believer, I must commit myself to pray for him.

Qualifications for fellowship

As you become convinced of the importance and necessity of spiritual fellowship with other believers on a close personal level, you will begin to ask, "Who can I have this kind of fellowship with?" It is obvious from what we have considered about mutual commitment, openness of sharing, and willingness to give and receive both encouragement and admonishment that you are not going to enter into this kind of relationship with just anyone in the Body of Christ. There are certain qualifications that both of you must meet. Here are some qualities to look for as you ask God for a bosom friend and then begin to look about to see whom He brings your way:

- A desire, backed up by action, to grow in

the Lord, both in personal character and in ministry to others.

- An ability to understand and identify with your needs, frustrations, and temptations, but in an objective way. We need understanding, but not pity.
- An ability to absolutely keep confidences so that you can share your inmost heart.
- A willingness to make a commitment toward your spiritual welfare.
- A mature recognition that he or she does not have all the answers for your life; a willingness to agonize, pray, and search the Scriptures with you for those answers.
- A willingness to be honest with you, not allowing you to continue unchallenged in a wrong attitude or action.

Those who are just beginning to grow in their Christian faith should look first for this kind of fellowship from someone who can disciple them on a one-to-one basis. A peer-level fellowship can be helpful to a young Christian for encouragement and prayer, but it should be accompanied by a fellowship environment that can provide a strong commitment to growth in understanding and application to the Scriptures. Christians who are more mature in the Lord will likely find their spiritual fellowship on a peer level with others of similar spiritual maturity.

Fellowship in small groups

Thus far our discussion of spiritual fellowship has focused primarily on a one-to-one relationship.

This, of course, is the most basic unit of spiritual fellowship, but not the only one. Another common fellowship unit is the small group. Most small groups today are organized around Bible study, with the members of the group seeking to learn together what a particular passage of Scripture teaches. Other small groups are called "care groups," where the objective is to share needs and pray for one another. Still other groups focus on accountability, keeping each other sharp in different areas of need. Ideally, fellowship groups should seek to incorporate all of these aspects: Bible study, sharing of needs, accountability, and prayer for one another.

I have already referred to the synergistic effect of two people sharing together what they have learned from Scripture. In a small group this can be greatly multiplied as more ideas are brought to bear on a passage. This assumes, of course, that each group member is depending on the Holy Spirit to open his understanding. Certainly we are going to gain no true insights into the Scriptures apart from His ministry, regardless of how we may stimulate one another's thinking.

There is a great deal of material in print about small groups; it is not the purpose of this book to go into detailed instruction about that material.[5] However, my own experience compels me to include this one word of caution: Great care should be taken to ensure that small groups do indeed accomplish the objective of spiritual fellowship, that is, of mutually enhancing our relationship with God. The dangers of spiritual pride over the knowledge we have gleaned from our Bible study and of playing one-upmanship are far greater in the small group than in a one-to-one relationship. There is also the danger of sharing strictly on an intellectual level rather than on the deeper heart level where God's Word is made applicable to our daily lives.

Spiritual fellowship becomes more and more difficult as a group becomes larger. There is obviously less intimacy and consequently less freedom to share with others what is really happening in our lives. An old Puritan adage addresses the importance of seeking to maintain fellowship with only a few in this manner: "Have communion with few, be intimate with *one*. Deal justly with all, speak evil of none."

The godly Puritans, who changed the face of English history amid unusual difficulties, realized the importance of genuine spiritual fellowship, the type mentioned by the writer of Hebrews. Most of the Puritan era was characterized by persecution of godly ministers and their ejection from their churches. They often ministered to their flocks in the woods outside the towns so as to avoid harassment from their enemies. It was vitally necessary in such difficult times for them to encourage each other and to spur each other on. Fellowship to them was no luxury; it was an urgent necessity.

We need to consider carefully, then, their advice about the *breadth* of fellowship. They realized that for fellowship to have depth in its meaning, it must be limited in its breadth: communion with a few, intimacy with one. Fellowship beyond the few tends to take on superficial characteristics, leading to little more than Christian social relationships that have erroneously become characterized as fellowship. Perhaps we need to take more literally the small number indicated by Jesus in that well-known passage, "Where two or three come together in my name, there am I with them" (Matthew 18:20). It is not, of course, that Christ is absent from us in our larger assemblies. Yet He does particularly emphasize in this statement the importance of the small fellowship group.

Your local body

It is obvious from Acts 2:42 that the early Church considered fellowship among the believers an important ingredient in their spiritual health, right along with hearing the Word of God and corporate prayer. Yet little attention seems to be given to this dimension of fellowship in our churches or other ministries today. We have meetings that emphasize the teaching of the Word and we sometimes have prayer meetings, but very little seems to be done to stimulate true spiritual fellowship. What often goes by the name of fellowship is simply social activity within the Body, an important activity but hardly answering the need of mutual spiritual stimulation.

The leaders of local churches and other Christian groups, then, need to give careful attention to the stimulation of true spiritual fellowship within their congregations and groups. The pattern of such fellowship may vary, but the objective of mutual spiritual uplifting and the principle of depth instead of breadth should be kept uppermost in mind. It is likely that the majority of Christians neither appreciate the importance of spiritual fellowship nor know how to go about it. They need both instruction and encouragement in the true biblical practice of koinonia.

One of the marks of a truly good church or Christian group on a campus or a military base should be the warmth of its spiritual fellowship. This aspect is just as important as the soundness of its teaching and the vitality of its outreach. Paul commended the believers at Rome because they were "full of goodness, complete in knowledge and competent to instruct one another" (Romans 15:14). They obviously engaged in spiritual fellowship, mutually building up and caring for one another.

God's delight in fellowship

Right at the end of the Old Testament we get a glimpse into the heart of God and His value of spiritual fellowship among believers. The setting is the nation of Israel in the process of being restored to its land by the Persian king, but falling again into a corrupt religious formality, neither worshiping nor obeying God. In fact many people of Israel were even saying that it was futile to serve God (Malachi 3:14-15).

Yet in the midst of that spiritual declension there was a group who feared the Lord and had fellowship together: "Those who feared the LORD talked with each other, and the LORD listened and heard. A scroll of remembrance was written in his presence concerning those who feared the LORD and honored his name" (Malachi 3:16). Two things are apparent from this passage concerning fellowship: (1) The godly Jews considered fellowship important. No doubt they had learned the vital necessity of encouraging one another in those difficult days of national backsliding. (2) But just as important is the clear indication of God's delight in their fellowship. He listened in on their times of fellowship, took special note of it, and even had a "scroll of remembrance" written in His presence concerning these godly people who sought to encourage one another and build each other up in the fear of the Lord.

The infinite, eternal mind of God obviously does not need a scroll of remembrance to remind Him of the gracious acts of His people. The allusion to such a scroll is for our benefit, that we might see the importance God places on true spiritual fellowship among His people and the delight it brings to His heart.

Notes

1. In Chapter 1, I used the word "communion" to describe this type of fellowship. But since that word today is most often associated with the Lord's Supper, I bow to common usage in this chapter and use "fellowship" to describe our sharing spiritually with one another.
2. Packer, *God's Words,* page 193.
3. Packer, page 200.
4. Packer, page 193.

5. NavPress publishes a periodical entitled *The Small Group Letter,* which covers a broad spectrum of the philosophy and methodology of small groups. For subscription information write: *The Small Group Letter*, Subscription Services, P.O. Box 53932, Boulder, CO 80322.

6
Partnership in the Gospel

I THANK MY GOD EVERY TIME
I REMEMBER YOU. IN ALL MY
PRAYERS FOR ALL OF YOU, I
ALWAYS PRAY WITH JOY
BECAUSE OF YOUR PARTNER-
SHIP IN THE GOSPEL FROM
THE FIRST DAY UNTIL NOW.

Philippians 1:3-5

The Apostle Paul wrote to the Philippian believers, "I thank my God . . . because of your partnership in the gospel from the first day until now" (Philippians 1:3-5). He considered those dear friends in Philippi to be actively engaged with him in the spreading of the gospel to other cities, even though most of them never left Philippi. As we saw in Chapter 1, the Greek word *koinōnia* is here translated as "partnership," the same as in a commercial business association.

When the word *koinōnia* is translated as "fellowship," we tend to think of a mutual enjoyment and building up of one another within the Body of Christ. It has an inward connotation that is very legitimate and necessary. Believers do need to be concerned for one another, to build up each other in the faith, and to enjoy each other's company. But we also recognize that the Christian must look outward to a chaotic world filled with sinners in need of a Savior. As we build up and enjoy one another, we are *in fellowship,* but as we join together to spread the gospel we are *in partnership;* our objectives are focused outside ourselves on those who need to be brought into the fellowship of God's people. It is in this sense that Paul regarded the Philippian believers as partners with him in the gospel.

Partnership in giving

Why did Paul rejoice so exuberantly in the partnership of the Philippians? How had they participated with him in his missionary enterprise when they had never even left home to go with him? A significant part of the answer to these questions is found in the fourth chapter of Philippians. Beginning at verse 10, Paul expresses heartfelt gratitude for the material gifts the Philippians had sent to him in Rome. Then in verse 15 he says, "When I set out from Macedonia, not one church shared with me in the matter of giving and receiving, except you only." Paul is emphasizing in this statement that the Philippian church was the only one that entered into *partnership* with him. That is actually what Paul is saying in this verse.

The Philippian believers had entered into partnership with Paul through their material assistance to him. They had done this from the earliest days of their acquaintance with the gospel.

The Philippians had apparently been taught that koinonia within the Christian community involved a *working* relationship. They recognized that they had a missionary responsibility to those cities beyond them and that one major way they could fulfill that responsibility was by giving to the ministry of the missionary Paul. They teamed up with Paul through their gifts to him.

Paul recognized their status as partners with him through their giving. He not only thanked God for their partnership but also assured them of a return on their investment. In verse 17 he says, "Not that I am looking for a gift, but I am looking for what may be credited to your account." He was confident that just as he would receive a reward for his labors, so the Philippians would share with him in that reward. Just as they had invested in his missionary enterprise as partners, so they would participate in the rewards of that enterprise as partners. Paul and the Philippians were truly partners in the gospel.

Every Christian today has the same privilege as did the believers at Philippi of being a partner in the gospel enterprise. Each of us has the opportunity to participate in ministries far beyond our own personal endeavors, both in cities at home and in countries overseas. Every time we give to a mission, either at home or overseas, we are joining in partnership with that particular ministry. And we will share in the fruit of that ministry in proportion to our sharing in its costs.

For many years I have had a deep concern for the peoples of Russia and China, perhaps because of the particularly oppressive anti-Christian regimes under which they live. Yet there is no way I can express that concern in person by going there. But there are ministries that do reach those peoples, both by sending missionaries on short-term visits and by reaching out to them through radio and literature. In giving to those ministries I enjoy the privilege of entering into a partnership with them in reaching the peoples of Russia and China, and I also expect to share in the fruits of their labors.

We have not only a *privilege* of partnership in the ministry; we have also a *responsibility*. Becoming partners in the gospel enterprise is not just an option for the committed Christian. Jesus said, "Go into all the world and preach the good news to all creation" (Mark 16:15). This is a command—not a suggestion or a request—that is repeated in all four Gospels and in the book of Acts. Our individual responsibility in fulfilling this command varies with the opportunities God gives us. But as we have opportunity, we should participate in the widest possible way in the spreading of the gospel to all the world.

Giving to missionary causes often seems to be presented as simply an option to Christians. Missionaries and prospective missionaries travel around to various churches presenting their ministries and requesting support. Each local church's missionary committee or individual members consider whether or not to give toward a missionary's support. The option is strictly with the giver, be it the church or its individual members. We tend to think we are being bighearted if we decide to give. In actuality we are not so much bighearted as we are obedient. Christ *commands* us to go into all the world, and the only way most of us can do that is by participating in the ministries of those who physically go.

Fellowship in this sense of partnership in the gospel is not so much an activity to be enjoyed as a responsibility to be fulfilled. Of course we will enjoy it as we share in the fruits of the partnership, but this enjoyment is secondary to our obedience to Christ's command to take the gospel to all creation. Partnership in the gospel through our giving is both a privilege and a duty.

Partnership in prayer

A second significant way in which we can enter into partnership in the gospel is through regular, meaningful prayer for those who are taking the gospel message beyond our own local church or fellowship. Again the Philippian believers are a beautiful example to us. They not only gave; they also prayed for Paul. And just as Paul expected results from their giving, so he also expected results from their prayers. He said, "I know that through your prayers and the help given by the Spirit of Jesus Christ, what has happened to me will turn out for my deliverance" (Philippians 1:19). Paul very much depended on the contribution to his ministry that these partners back in Philippi provided through their prayers.

On seven different occasions in his letters to the various churches, Paul either requested prayer for his ministry or acknowledged that his readers were praying for him. To Paul their prayers were more important than their gifts. He could get along without their gifts (see Philippians 4:11-13), but he could not get along without their prayers. His succinct request, "Brothers, pray for us" (1 Thessalonians 5:25), sums up Paul's sense of urgency for believers to join him in his ministry by praying for him.

It is very likely that Christians in the historic missionary-sending countries have neglected the prayer aspect of partnership in the gospel even more than they have neglected participation by giving. Too often the missionary is "out of sight, out of mind." We may set up a giving program, either through our church or an independent agency, so that we do give regularly to the missionary enterprise. This is a positive step that should be taken. But are we as faithful to pray as we are to give? If we are truly to be partners in the gospel, we must commit ourselves to pray for missionaries—as well as for pastors and evangelists in our own country—in a consistent, meaningful way.

Every missionary, either at home or abroad, and every mission agency that our family gives to, is listed on my personal prayer list and is prayed for on a regular basis. We cannot leave this part of our responsibility to chance. In order to be true partners in prayer, we must structure our schedules and our prayer lives in a way that fulfills our responsibility in the partnership. And again, as in our responsibility to participate through giving, this responsibility is not an option. If we intend to be obedient to Christ's command to go into all the world, the issue is not whether to pray but simply where our particular responsibility lies. What missionaries or what agencies has God assigned to us as our responsibility in partnership through our prayers?

Not only should our partnership in prayer be consistent; it should also be meaningful. That is, our prayers should get beyond the general by addressing specific needs and opportunities that our missionary partners are facing. Paul was very specific in his request for prayer help from the church at Rome. He wrote to them, "I urge you, brothers, by our Lord Jesus Christ and by the love of the Spirit, to join me in my struggle by praying to God for me. Pray that I may be rescued from the unbelievers in Judea and that my service in Jerusalem may be acceptable to the saints there" (Romans 15:30-31).

Paul requested prayer for his own personal protection (that he might be rescued from unbelievers) and for success in a specific ministry (that his service might be acceptable to the saints). He made a similar request for prayer to the Thessalonian Christians: "Pray for us that the message of the Lord may spread rapidly . . . and pray that we may be delivered from wicked and evil men" (2 Thessalonians 3:1-2).

A brief look at Paul's appeals for prayer shows an approximately equal division between requests for his personal needs and requests for his ministry. This should give us a general sense of balance as we pray for missionaries today. Missionaries and their families have personal needs—loneliness, cultural adjustment, protection from harm, and health care—but they also have ministry needs. I have observed in prayer meetings that when we pray for missionaries, we tend to focus on their personal needs. The reason, of course, is that we can more easily identify with those particular needs. But if we truly want to be partners with them in their ministries, we must also join with them in praying for their ministry needs.

Paul requested prayer for such things as boldness in sharing Christ, for the right words to speak, for open doors to proclaim the gospel, and for the rapid spread of the gospel (Ephesians 6:19, Colossians 4:3-4, 2 Thessalonians 3:1). Today's missionaries have the same ministry needs as did Paul. They also need boldness in sharing Christ, wisdom for the best way to do it, and open doors of opportunity.

One of the most critical needs, however, is found in the instruction of Jesus, who told His disciples to pray for workers to go into the harvest field (Matthew 9:38). Perhaps the most pressing need on the mission field today is for God to raise up workers from within the ranks of each country's own people. Consequently, the most urgent task of the missionary today is training workers from the country where he is working. We ought to pray to this end. In fact this particular prayer request—for God to raise up national workers—is my number-one prayer request as I pray for missions and missionaries around the world.

While writing this chapter, I received a prayer letter from a missionary friend who quoted S. D. Gordon on the importance of prayer for missions. Here is what Gordon said:

> The greatest thing each one of us can do is to pray. If we can go personally to some distant land, still we have gone to only one place.
>
> Prayer puts us into direct dynamic touch with a world. A man may go aside today, and shut the door, and as really spend a half-hour of his life in India for God as though he were there in person. Surely you and I must get more half-hours for this secret service.

My missionary friend goes on in his letter to emphasize that it is not only the half hours that count. He says, "The few-minute sessions that you invest for people and needs overseas can also have a large impact. A half-dozen such sessions during the day add up and mean much in other parts of the world, opening hearts and thwarting Satan's attacks."

As a former short-term missionary, I can personally testify to the importance of prayer partners back home. I still remember a particular weekend when I was struggling desperately with discouragement and depression. On Sunday evening the depression suddenly lifted. Several weeks later I learned that friends back home had specially prayed for me that day and that at that precise time, God answered their prayer.

William Carey of England, who has been

called "the father of modern missions," went to India in 1793. At that time there were no organized missionary societies, but as Carey prayed over the needs of an unreached world, God laid India on his heart. At a "commissioning" service for Carey and his colleague in March, 1793, one of Carey's friends exclaimed, "There is a gold mine in India but it seems almost as deep as the centre of the earth!" to which Carey replied, "I will venture down but remember that you must hold the ropes."[1]

How did Carey expect his friends to "hold the ropes"? It was to be through a partnership in prayer and in giving. Those who hold the ropes are just as important in the partnership as those who go down into the mine. Holding the ropes for others is a significant part of biblical fellowship; it is essential for the spread of the gospel.

Notes

1. Mary Drewery, *William Carey* (Grand Rapids: Zondervan, 1979), page 46. According to Drewery, the quote is not exact but is the gist of what was said.

7
The Fellowship of Spiritual Gifts

EACH ONE SHOULD USE
WHATEVER GIFT HE HAS
RECEIVED TO SERVE OTHERS,
FAITHFULLY ADMINISTERING
GOD'S GRACE IN ITS VARIOUS
FORMS.

1 Peter 4:10

At the time of our conversion, God incorporates us into the Body of Christ. He places us in a community relationship with all other believers in which we together share a common life in Christ. This is an objective fact; we *are* in fellowship with all other believers. This objective aspect of fellowship, however, is intended to provide a basis for experiential fellowship. We are not meant to be passive participants or, to use a business metaphor, silent partners in the partnership of the gospel. Rather, God intends for all Christians to be active participants in the Body, working partners in the enterprise of the gospel.

To this end God has assigned to every Christian a function in the Body of Christ. There are no exceptions to this; every member has a function within the Body that God has assigned him to fulfill. Warren Myers, in his book *Pray: How to Be Effective in Prayer,* tells of two remarkable people: William Carey, missionary to India, and Carey's bedridden, almost totally paralyzed sister. William Carey accomplished a Bible translation work unequaled in missionary history and, as we saw in the last chapter, he has been called "the father of modern missions." We don't even know his sister's name. She is mentioned only as Carey's sister. But while Carey labored in India translating and printing parts or all of the Bible into forty languages, his sister lay on her back in London and prayed hour after hour, month after month, for all the details, problems, and struggles of her brother's work. In telling this story of Carey and his sister, Myers asks the question, "To whose account will God credit the victories won through this remarkable man?"[1] We all know that Carey's sister shared in his ministry. In fact, she was a very vital part. Without her ministry of intercession on her brother's behalf, the work would not have gone forward.

Function in the Body

The point of the above story is to emphasize that God assigns to *every* believer an important function in the Body. He assigned William Carey to do Bible translation work in India and He assigned his sister to pray for that work as she lay paralyzed in her bed in London. William Carey's function was highly visible, at least it is to us today; his sister's function was probably unknown except to a few people. Yet both had a vital part to play in the missionary enterprise in India. God assigned each of them a specific function and enabled them by His grace to fulfill it.

Just as God assigns to each of us a function in the Body of Christ, so He equips each of us to fulfill that function. In the New Testament this equipping is called a "gift." *A spiritual gift is an ability given by God and empowered by the Holy Spirit to perform the specific function within the Body that God has assigned to each of us.* Spiritual gifts are distinct from natural abilities, although the gifts frequently incorporate some natural ability. While both gifts and abilities are endowments from God, gifts are related specifically to the function God has assigned to us in the Body.

In his discourse on spiritual gifts in Romans 12:3-8, Paul, using the analogy of the physical body, said, "Just as each of us has one body with many members, and these members do not all have the same function, so in Christ we who are many form one body. . . . We have different gifts, according to the grace given us" (12:4,6). Note the relationship between function and gift. We all have different functions, and consequently different gifts that enable us to fulfill those functions.

In the last couple of decades, quite an emphasis has been placed on spiritual gifts, especially on the aspect of discovering what one's particular gift is. Unfortunately, not enough emphasis has been placed on discovering what one's *function* is in the Body. Gifts are given by God to enable us to fulfill our function. As Peter said in 1 Peter 4:10, "Each one should use whatever gift he has received to serve others, faithfully administering God's grace in its various forms." And Paul spoke similarly of the communal significance of a gift when he said, "Now to each one the manifestation of the Spirit is given for the common good" (1 Corinthians 12:7). Gifts are to be used to serve others; they are given for the common good of the whole Body. Their purpose is to enable us to fulfill our function.

Many people these days are wondering what their gift is, but they are not finding the answer because they are asking the wrong question. We should be seeking primarily to find out our function in the Body: the particular task assigned by God. We may be sure that God has equipped us, both in natural ability and in spiritual gifts, for the function He has called us to perform.

Over the years I have concluded that my gifts are in the areas of administration and teaching, but I did not realize this at the beginning of my Christian experience. I entered full-time vocational Christian work at the age of twenty-five, and for a number of years I simply worked at the tasks God gave me to do in The Navigators. Later I concluded, in retrospect, that God had given me the gift of administration because He had always assigned me to that type of ministry in The Navigators and had always enabled me to perform it. In the same way I concluded that God had also given me the gift of teaching because I consistently found myself doing it and experiencing God's blessing on my efforts.

But the important fact to note is that I had been performing the functions of administration and teaching long before I recognized these as gifts God had given. God had assigned me to the functions of administration and teaching, He had equipped me through spiritual gifts to do them, and He had providentially arranged the circumstances of my life so that I actually performed those functions. Our gifts are always consistent with our functions.

In defining the broad areas of fellowship as it is described in the New Testament, I have used the words "participation" and "partnership," both valid translations of the Greek word *koinōnia.* If we view the Church of Jesus Christ as His *Body,* then we recognize that we are participants, sharing together a common life in Christ and using our spiritual gifts to serve each other, symbiotically building us up in the faith. The Church is a spiritual enterprise engaged in carrying out Christ's Great Commission to make disciples in all nations. We have been called by God to be a team of dedicated partners actively involved in that effort.

Whether fellowship is perceived as participation or partnership, in either case it implies a responsibility to fulfill our function in the Body. We usually don't think of fellowship in terms of fulfilling a responsibility, but that is because we have lost sight of the biblical meaning of fellowship. Fellowship is not just a social privilege to enjoy; it is more basically a responsibility to assume.

Sharing our spiritual gifts

Koinonia can also mean to share what we have with others. Two areas of sharing specifically mentioned in the Bible are those of spiritual truths and material possessions. But we are also called to share with others the benefits of our spiritual gifts. We are to use them, as Peter said, to serve others. So whether we think of fellowship as a sharing together in a joint participation or a sharing of what we have with others, we find that fellowship involves the use of the gifts God has given us.

I have entitled this chapter "The Fellowship of Spiritual Gifts." This probably sounds strange to those accustomed to thinking of fellowship as Christian social activity or the sharing of spiritual truths. But when we see that fellowship is a sharing together or a sharing with, it makes sense. The fellowship of our spiritual gifts is the using of our gifts for the benefit of the rest of the Body and for the advancement of the Kingdom of God.

Principles of spiritual gifts

Having seen that biblical fellowship involves the use of our spiritual gifts to fulfill our function in the Body, we need to consider certain basic truths or principles regarding spiritual gifts.

(1) *The purpose of all spiritual gifts is to serve others and to glorify God.* Consider again 1 Peter 4:10, along with verse 11: "Each one should use whatever gift he has received to serve others . . . so that in all things God may be praised through Jesus Christ." According to Peter, there are two objectives in the use of our gifts: serving others

and glorifying or praising God. He also referred to us as stewards in the use of our gifts: "Employ [your gift] in serving one another, as good stewards of the manifold grace of God" (1 Peter 4:10, NASB). When used in this sense, "steward" refers to a person who manages someone else's property, finances, or other affairs. Our gifts are not our property to use as we please; they are a trust committed to us by God to use for others and for His glory as He directs.

There is no place in the use of spiritual gifts for the seeking of recognition, fame, or self-fulfillment. It is true that some gifts by their nature bring recognition or fame more so than others. In his classic treatment on spiritual gifts in 1 Corinthians 12, Paul recognizes this fact. He sees that just as there is a hierarchy of influence and strength among the parts of the physical body, so there is among the members of Christ's Body. But the fact that this is true is no excuse for us to covet recognition, or to use our gifts in such a way as to gain it. God gives recognition to whomever He is pleased to give it. Two men may be equally gifted in teaching the Word of God. But God assigns one man to a large pulpit and radio ministry while He assigns the other man to a one-on-one discipling situation or a small Sunday school class. One gets recognition and fame; the other is unknown beyond his small sphere of ministry.

Some gifts by their nature are more public than others and thus they are more prone to result in recognition. This would be true, for example, of the gifts of teaching and service. In our church there are those of us who exercise the gift of teaching. We are frequently before our Sunday school classes or Bible study groups. Everyone knows who we are. There are others who exercise the gift of service in seeing that the physical aspects of the church are in place and properly functioning for the rest of us. Hardly anyone ever sees the work that they do. In fact, as long as they do their job properly, few people even think about it; their work is taken for granted by most of the congregation.

As long as we keep in mind the purpose of gifts, however, we will not be concerned about recognition or fame. We will seek to use our gifts as stewards entrusted with the grace of God to be used to serve others and to glorify Him. Whether ours is a public gift like teaching or a less noticeable gift like serving, the end objective is "that in all things God may be praised through Jesus Christ."

(2) *Every Christian has a gift and every gift is important.* We have already stated earlier in this chapter that God has assigned every believer a function in the Body of Christ and that God has consequently gifted every member to fulfill that function. We need to underscore this point. God has given a spiritual gift to every individual believer in the Body of Christ. Paul expressly says, "Now to each one the manifestation of the Spirit is given for the common good" (1 Corinthians 12:7). It is important that we acknowledge this fact because so many Christians seem to have the attitude that they do not have a gift. They may have this attitude because they secretly covet a public

gift that might bring recognition or because they have an overly restrictive view of spiritual gifts that keeps them from recognizing, for example, that their ability to show compassion to the needy, the suffering, or the unlovely is actually the important gift of mercy.

To say "I don't think I have a gift" is to say "I don't think I have a function in the Body of Christ." Such an idea flies in the face of the whole of New Testament teaching. God has a job for every believer. It may be seen or unseen, big or small, but each of us has a job to do.

Not only do we each have a gift; each one of our gifts is important. Again we tend to recognize the more public, noticeable gifts as important and the low profile gifts as perhaps not so important. The Apostle Paul anticipates this tendency when he envisions the foot saying, "Because I am not a hand, I do not belong to the body," and the ear saying, "Because I am not an eye, I do not belong to the body" (1 Corinthians 12:15-16). Here Paul has in mind the person with the less noticeable gift comparing himself with the person with the more noticeable gift, and then feeling that he has no gift at all. I believe this is a very common tendency among Christians today, particularly among those who have the gifts of serving others in practical ways, such as through hospitality or meeting the temporal needs of others in the Body.

Of course there is also a danger that those with the more public gifts will secretly disregard or belittle the contribution to the Body of those who have the less noticeable gifts. Again Paul anticipates this tendency in 1 Corinthians 12:21 when he says, "The eye cannot say to the hand, 'I don't need you!' And the head cannot say to the feet, 'I don't need you!'" We all need each other's contribution in the Body. Just as some functions in the human body are in a sense more important than others, so it is with some gifts in the Body of Christ. Paul seems to recognize this in verses 28 31 of 1 Corinthians 12. But this does not change the fact that *all* gifts are important. Some are more important than others, perhaps, but none are unimportant. So whether we have the less important or the more important gifts, let us not envy one or despise the other. We need to recognize that each gift is necessary in the Body and is important to God.

(3) *Gifts are sovereignly bestowed by God.* Just as God assigns us certain functions in the Body, so He bestows our gifts. Speaking of gifts in 1 Corinthians 12:11, Paul says, "All these are the work of one and the same Spirit, and he gives them to each man, just as he determines." Again using the physical body as an analogy, Paul states in verse 18, "God has arranged the parts in the body, every one of them, just as he wanted them to be." The obvious inference is that just as God sovereignly arranged the parts of the physical body, so He sovereignly arranged us as individual parts in the Body of Christ.

Perhaps this principle seems too obvious to state. But consider the implications and the applications of this principle. You possess the gifts you have because the sovereign God of the universe wanted you to be that way. He ordained a plan for your life before you were even born, and He has gifted you specifically to carry out that plan.

Never disparage your gift. If you do, you are disparaging the plan of God and perhaps complaining against Him. Similarly, never look down on the gift of another. If you do, you are scorning the plan of God for that person.

God not only determines what gift (or gifts[2]) each of us has; He also determines the measure or extent of that gift. Two people may have the same gift, but in different measure. Earlier I referred to the possibility of two teachers of the Word equally gifted, one laboring in obscurity and the other enjoying widespread recognition. While I recognize such realities in the functioning of the Body, I believe the usual explanation is that two people are gifted in a certain area but that one is more gifted than the other. Both gifts are being carried out under the sovereign providence of God.

Jesus spoke of three servants receiving different amounts of "talents," each according to his ability (Matthew 25:14-30). A biblical "talent" was not a mental or physical ability but an amount of money something more than a thousand dollars. Each of the servants was to invest a certain sum of money in order to earn interest. Apparently each servant had the same calling to invest money. But they had different degrees of ability within that calling, and so they received different degrees of responsibility according to their abilities.

It is the same way with spiritual gifts. God gives us not only the particular gift we have, but also the measure of that gift. Then He holds us responsible to use our gift to its full measure. The person who has a greater measure of a certain gift has greater responsibility for it. "From everyone who has been given much, much will be demanded" (Luke 12:48). The three servants in the parable of the talents were judged not in relation to each other but according to how they used what had been entrusted to them.

(4) *Every gift is given by God's grace.* The Greek word for a spiritual gift is *charisma,* which means "a gift of God's *grace,*" whether it is the gift of eternal life as in Romans 6:23, or the gift of a spiritual ability for use in the Body.

Paul said, "We have different gifts, according to the *grace* given us," and Peter said, "Each one should use whatever gift he has received to serve others, faithfully administering God's *grace* in its various forms" (Romans 12:6, 1 Peter 4:10, italics added). None of us deserves the gift he or she has been given. All the gifts are given by God's undeserved favor on us through Christ.

In Ephesians 3:7-8, Paul testified freely that he did not deserve to be an apostle of Jesus Christ: "I became a servant of this gospel by the gift of God's grace given me through the working of his power. Although I am less than the least of all God's people, this grace was given me: to preach to the Gentiles the unsearchable riches of Christ."

According to this principle, the most worthy and the most unworthy of all Christians both receive their gifts on the same basis. The unworthy person surely does not deserve his gift, but neither does the most worthy. They both receive them as unmerited favors from God. The highly gifted person should not think he is so gifted because of his hard work or his faithfulness in previous service to God. Likewise, the person who feels he has wasted a good part of his life and is consequently undeserving of any spiritual gift should not despair. Paul said he received his gift despite the fact that he was the least of all God's people. Worthy or unworthy, it makes no difference. All gifts are given by God's grace.

(5) *All gifts must be developed and exercised.* Even though gifts are given by God's grace, it is our responsibility to develop and exercise them. Paul exhorted Timothy to rekindle or "fan into flame the gift of God," and elsewhere Paul told him, "Do not neglect your gift" (2 Timothy 1:6, 1 Timothy 4:14).

In order to effectively exercise our spiritual gifts, even though they are sovereignly and graciously bestowed, we must develop and use them. The effective use of our gifts does not occur without diligent effort on our part. Timothy already had the gift of teaching, yet Paul did not hesitate to urge him to be diligent to present himself to God as a workman who could correctly handle the Word of Truth. And in 1 Timothy, after exhorting Timothy not to neglect his gift, Paul said, "Be diligent in these matters; give yourself wholly to them" (1 Timothy 4:15). Timothy's use of his gift was not a matter of indifference. He was accountable to a sovereign God for his development and use of it.

This means hard work. The person with the

gift of teaching must study zealously to learn God's truth and must then labor diligently to communicate it in a clear and inspiring manner. The person with the gift of service must strive to become competent and proficient in his particular area of service in order to ensure that the results of his labors reflect a standard of excellence that glorifies God. There is no place for either shoddy teaching or shoddy service in God's Kingdom.

The believer with the gift of mercy must study how to use that gift in a way that best relieves the sufferings and miseries of others. The person who has the gift of leadership must study the principles of leadership in order to use his gift most effectively, and then, as Paul said, he must govern diligently. Simply having a spiritual gift does not mean we can automatically fulfill our function in the Body without diligent effort. Rather, we are responsible to develop and use the gifts God has given us.

(6) *The effective use of every gift is dependent on faith in Christ.* Although gifts are sovereignly bestowed and although their effective exercise involves hard work and diligent effort, it is also true that no gift is exercised apart from faith in Christ. We cannot assume God's blessing on our efforts even though we are laboring within the bounds of the gifts He has given us. The necessity of conscious dependence on Christ for His enabling power is a fundamental fact for every aspect of the Christian life, whether in spiritual growth in our own lives or in service within the Body. "Apart from me," Jesus said, "you can do nothing" (John 15:5).

Speaking of his own diligent efforts, Paul wrote to the believers at Colosse, "To this end I labor, struggling with all [Christ's] energy, which so powerfully works in me" (Colossians 1:29). Paul labored diligently in the exercising of his gifts. In fact, as we have already seen, he described his labor as "struggling." Yet he also relied on Christ. The persevering apostle struggled with the energy that Christ infused in him as he labored in dependence on Him.

To maintain the proper perspective of diligent personal responsibility and a sincere attitude of total dependence on Christ for His power requires constant vigilance in two directions. On the one hand, we can be guilty of slothfulness in the development or use of our gifts under the pretext that we are "trusting in the Lord." On the other hand, we can either presume on God's blessing as we attempt to use our gifts in the strength of our own abilities or assert the fact that we have "done that so many times."

I personally find it easier to consciously acknowledge my dependence on Christ in the area of teaching than in the area of administration. Teaching spiritual truth from the Bible is obviously spiritual work requiring divine enabling. Administration, which for me means the business affairs of The Navigators, is not so obviously spiritual. The temptation is to rely on my training, experience, or "practical wisdom" rather than on God. It is quite instructive, however, to note that in his admonition regarding the use of our gifts, Peter expressly says, "If anyone serves, he should do it with the strength God provides" (1 Peter 4:11). The gift of service is usually associated with physical and material needs within the Body. Yet the meeting of those physical needs requires God's strength just as much as the meeting of spiritual needs in the Body. Truly, without Christ we can do nothing.

(7) *Only love will give true value to our gifts.* In any discussion of spiritual gifts we should give careful attention to the fact that the classic Scripture passage on Christian love, 1 Corinthians 13, is set right in the middle of the Bible's most extensive treatment on spiritual gifts. In the first part of chapter 13, Paul tells us that even if we possess the greatest of gifts, have the most extraordinary faith, and display an amazing amount of zeal and courage yet have not love, we are nothing and we accomplish nothing.

It is not that Paul sets love over against spiritual gifts or Christian zeal as if love is more important than gifts, faith, or zeal. Rather, he says that it is love that gives all these other areas value and worth. The gifts and character traits Paul mentions in 1 Corinthians 13:1-3 are not insignificant or commonplace. Whatever we may think about the bestowal and use of some of these gifts today, the fact is that in Paul's day the gifts of tongues and prophecy were the most coveted of gifts. And who of us would not desire the faith that can move mountains, or the sacrificial spirit that would prompt us to give our goods to the poor, or the spiritual courage that enables martyrs to endure the flames?

Yet Paul very plainly says, not once but three times, that only love gives value to our gifts, our faith, and our zeal. If we set our hearts only on the exercising of our gifts, the increase of our faith, and the promotion of our zeal and courage, without seeking to grow in love, we will be as nothing and accomplish nothing. We may generate a lot of Christian activity, gain some measure of fame, and even appear to accomplish something for God. But if we have not love, it all amounts to nothing.

Write down, either in your imagination or on a sheet of paper, a row of zeros. Keep adding zeros until you have filled a whole line on the page. What do they add up to? Exactly nothing! Even if you were to write a thousand of them, they would still be nothing. But put a positive number in front of them and immediately they have value. This is the way it is with our gifts and faith and zeal. They are the zeros on the page. Without love, they count for nothing. But put love in front of them and immediately they have value.[3] And just as the number two gives more value to a row of zeros than the number one does, so more and more love can add exponentially greater value to our gifts.

Notice how Paul describes love in 1 Corinthians 13:4-7. Each description of it is in the arena of interpersonal relationships. We would expect from the larger context that Paul might want to instruct us on how to prophesy in love, how to exercise faith in love, and how to give sacrificially in love, but he does not do that. Instead he talks about exercising patience and being kind to one another. He talks about love eliminating envy and boasting, rudeness and selfishness. He says that love is not easily angered and keeps no record of wrongs. Paul has thus passed from the subject of gifts to the subject of relationships.

What is Paul saying to *us* through this subtle change in subject matter? Just this: Love must permeate and govern every aspect of our lives. Love is not to be exercised only in the use of our gifts and in the performance of our various Christian duties. Love is to be exercised in the home, or at the office, or in the classroom, where our gifts are not a particular consideration. Love is to be exercised all the time in the most mundane duties of life, not just when we are engaged in Christian work. On the other hand, the absence of love in the ordinary duties and relationships of life can undermine and destroy the effective use of our gifts.

This is not a book on love or even on gifts, but a book on *fellowship*—a sharing together of the life we have in common in Jesus Christ. It is love that, practically speaking, enables us to share together that life. It is the cement of love that binds together those living stones that are being built into a spiritual house. Love is the ligament that binds the members into one Body. And though our gifts are important in the *functioning* of the Body, it is love that gives *unity* to the Body and makes that functioning effective.

Therefore, any consideration of gifts must include the importance of love. We all believe this, but we often fail to practice it. We often place people in Christian organizations on the basis of gifts and other abilities with little regard to their ability to love. Pulpit committees screening pastoral candidates give great attention to preaching ability and counseling skill, but seldom ever ask, "Does he exhibit love in the home, or toward the custodian and secretary at the church?" Most of our discipleship training, whether on the university campus, on the military base, or in the local church, emphasizes training in ministry skills. While this is certainly important, we must not neglect growth in love. I remember hearing of one university student of whom it was said, "He can lead people to Christ, but no one wants to room with him." Whether he could, given that immaturity of character, truly lead people to a saving knowledge of Christ may be questioned by some. But whether he could or not, it is true that a great big dose of love was needed to make him truly effective.

And so it is with all of us. We must seek to diligently exercise the gifts that God has graciously given to us. We must do so with faith in Christ in order to make them fruitful. But in both the use of our spiritual gifts and the exercise of our Christian ministries, we must seek to grow in love toward one another. Otherwise, when the final chapter of our lives has been penned, we will have to write a final line: "I have gained nothing."

Recognizing your gifts

As we truly commit ourselves to do God's will, we may be sure that He will so direct the course of our lives that we will begin to exercise our spiritual gifts and fulfill our function in the Body of Christ.

Throughout the course of time, however, it is important for us to periodically evaluate how God has directed our lives in service to others in the Body. If we are to develop our gifts, we must know what they are. Additionally, it seems to be the common experience of most Christians that God's way of directing their lives changes as they mature in Christ.

When we are spiritually young Christians, God usually directs us into His particular will for our lives through very clear providential circumstances or through rather strong subjective indications of His will. When we are spiritually immature, we must be led just as a child is led down a busy street by an adult. As we mature in the Lord, however, we find our subjective perceptions of God's will to be much less frequent and His particular will for us more difficult to determine. It is at this time that our awareness of what particular gifts God has given us can help us determine His specific will for us at certain times of decision-making. One of the most significant career decisions I ever made was reached primarily on the basis of my spiritual gifts, which were more suited to one option than to another. Recognition and understanding of your spiritual gifts should be a crucial factor in deciding God's leading in the major decisions of your life.

Paul urged us to assess our gifts in Romans 12:3 when he said, "By the grace given me I say to every one of you: Do not think of yourself more highly than you ought, but rather think of yourself with sober judgment, in accordance with the measure of faith God has given you." The context of this passage indicates that this is a call to serious assessment of our spiritual gifts. How, then, should we evaluate God's leading in our lives and recognize the gifts that He has given to us for the good of the Body?

Although no pat formula can be given, there are several suggestions that may be helpful in assessing our gifts. First, we must be sure that we are committed to doing the will of God that He has ordained for us. It's been said that ninety percent of finding God's will lies in our willingness to do it. Since God's will for us is consistent with His gifts to us, we may also say that a commitment to do whatever God wants us to do is necessary in determining what our gifts are. Note, however, that this willingness is a willingness to *do* God's will and a willingness to fulfill our function in the Body. It is not a willingness to find out something about ourselves, that is, to find out what our gifts are. Rather, it is a willingness to do whatever God has appointed us to do in the Body of Christ.

Assuming that you have already committed yourself to doing the will of God, consider then how He has providentially led you. What has He given you to do, and, of equal importance, what has He *not* given you to do? What service in the Body have you tried in which you have experienced His blessings on your efforts? What things have you tried in which you have not experienced His blessing? What opportunities to serve have been opened to you? What opportunities have in some way been closed to you?

At one important decision juncture in my life a ministry opportunity that I was quite excited about was closed to me because there was no one to replace me in my existing responsibilities. Just a few months later, however, a replacement was available and I was asked to take an altogether different type of assignment. Later on it became clear to me that the first opportunity lay outside the realm of my gifts, while the eventual assignment was consistent with them. This major incident, along with others, helped me recognize what gifts I have and, just as importantly, what gifts I do not have.

Consider also your natural abilities and your temperament. While natural abilities are not the same as spiritual gifts, it is true that spiritual gifts build on some of our abilities and temperament traits. For example, I have mentioned that I consider myself to have the gift of teaching. The gift of teaching assumes, among other things, the ability to study and to organize the fruit of the study. I have always been a natural student, both by intellect and by temperament. I am much more comfortable with ideas and concepts than with tools and building materials. The gifts of both administration and teaching build on my natural ability and temperament.

One word of caution is needed at this point: Natural abilities and temperaments are not always a sure indicator of gifts. Many natural abilities in music and various creative skills have been buried out on a mission field because the person was called by God to a pioneer missionary endeavor.

Our abilities and even our temperaments have to be laid at the foot of the Cross and left there for God to either take up and use in our lives or, if He so chooses, to leave lying at the foot of the Cross.

Perhaps the most crucial and telling criterion for assessing your gift is the confirmation from other Christians. The exercising of your spiritual gift should result in ministry and blessing to others. They can tell if you have ministered to them. If you have, they will let you know, either by words of appreciation and encouragement or by requests for you to minister to them again. Finally, you might seek confirmation of what you believe your gifts to be from Christians you respect, people who know you well enough to help you in your evaluation.

Whatever your gifts are, you may be sure that when you exercise them you will find joy and fulfillment as you share with others in the Body the gifts God has given you.

Notes

1. Warren Myers, *Pray: How to Be Effective in Prayer* (Colorado Springs: NavPress, 1983), page xvii.
2. There seems to be disagreement among Bible scholars on whether a person may have more than one gift. I personally believe in the affirmative, but the issue is not crucial to this discussion. In the text, I use gift or gifts without any particular significance between singular or plural.
3. I am indebted to J. D. Jones (1865-1942) for this illustration taken, though not quoted verbatim,

from his book *An Exposition of First Corinthians 13,* originally published in 1925 by Hodder & Stoughton of London and republished in 1982 by Klock & Klock Christian Publishers, Inc., Minneapolis.

8
Sharing Your Possessions

DO NOT FORGET TO DO GOOD
AND TO SHARE WITH OTHERS,
FOR WITH SUCH SACRIFICES
GOD IS PLEASED.

Hebrews 13:16

Before me on my desk lies a financial appeal from a Christian organization that specializes in assisting national Christian workers overseas. Every week I receive letters from organizations that reach out to ghetto children in the United States or feed starving people in drought-stricken countries overseas. The requests for funds to support these various ministries seem endless, as in fact they are, because the needs themselves are endless.

What biblical responsibility does a believer have to respond to the material needs of other people or to support organizations that specialize in meeting those kinds of needs? Has God given instructions in His Word that can guide the Christian in these situations, or is everyone left to his own sense of charity and benevolence? And exactly what does this subject of giving have to do with fellowship?

An analysis of the various ways *koinōnia* is used in the New Testament reveals that its most common usage is to indicate the sharing of possessions with those in need. This is a rather startling fact when we consider that today the most common concepts of fellowship deal with Christian social activity or sharing with one another on a spiritual level. As we reflect, however, on the first meaning of koinonia that we looked at in Chapter 1—that fellowship denotes primarily a community relationship of all believers—it should not surprise us that one of the principal means of expressing that relationship is through sharing our material goods with those in need. This practical demonstration of care and concern for other members of the Body of Christ is a very important expression of New Testament fellowship.

In order to appreciate this emphasis on sharing financially with those in need, it will be helpful to look at a list of Scripture passages that translate *koinōnia* in this manner. The italicized words in the following verses are all translations of the word *koinōnia* in either noun or verb form:

> *Share* with God's people who are in need. Practice hospitality. (Romans 12:13)

> Macedonia and Achaia were pleased to make *a contribution* for the poor among the saints in Jerusalem. They were pleased to do it, and

> indeed they owe it to them. For if the Gentiles have *shared* in the Jews' spiritual blessings, they owe it to the Jews to share with them their material blessings. (Romans 15:26-27)

> They urgently pleaded with us for the privilege of *sharing* in this service to the saints. (2 Corinthians 8:4)

> Because of the service by which you have proved yourselves, men will praise God for the obedience that accompanies your confession of the gospel of Christ, and for your generosity in *sharing* with them and with everyone else. (2 Corinthians 9:13)

> Command them to do good, to be rich in good deeds, and to be generous and *willing to share.* (1 Timothy 6:18)

> Do not forget to do good and *to share* with others, for with such sacrifices God is pleased. (Hebrews 13:16)

Sharing: An act of obedience

These verses set out in this manner should help us appreciate the force of the New Testament teaching on sharing materially with those in need as an expression of fellowship. As we consider these passages, two truths readily stand out. First, we are *commanded* to share with those in need and, second, it is a *joy* to share our possessions with others.

Too often, it seems, the act of giving to those in need is presented as an optional matter. Heartrending needs of homeless children and starving tribes are presented to us to arouse our compassion and to appeal to our sense of benevolence. The most heartrending story carries the day, and hopefully elicits a response from our checkbook. While such needs should stir up pity and compassion within us, this should not be our primary motivation for giving. Rather, the primary motive should be that of obedience to God.

Consider the following expressions from the Apostle Paul taken from the above passages: "[The Gentiles] *owe* it to the Jews to share with them. . . ." "Men will praise God for the *obedience* [of giving] that accompanies your confession. . . ." "Command them . . . to be . . . willing to share."

We are commanded to share; it is an act of obedience; we owe it to those in need to share with them. This expression of fellowship is not an option drawn from our feelings of pity and compassion. It is a duty commanded by God, arising out of the nature of fellowship as a community relationship. For the Christian who seeks to obey all the will of God, such sharing is simply an expression of obedience to his Lord.

We must wean ourselves from the attitude that giving to those in need is something that we may or may not do, depending on our feelings. The issue is not whether to give but rather what needs, of all those that come to our attention, we should respond to.

Of course an awareness of those in material

need should arouse a sense of compassion within us. The Apostle John said, "If anyone has material possessions and sees his brother in need but has no pity on him, how can the love of God be in him?" (1 John 3:17). This is a serious question. John is essentially questioning the profession of faith of those whose hearts are not moved enough to respond to those in need. Since it is the Holy Spirit who has created the fellowship of community among believers, we may be sure that He will create within the members of the community a care and concern for one another and a compassion for those members in need.

In Romans 12:13 Paul said, "Share with God's people who are in need." John Murray offered a very instructive interpretation of this verse:

> It is true that if we comply with this exhortation we shall distribute and impart our possessions to meet the needs of the saints. But though this is implied as a consequence the precise thought does not appear to be that of [sharing with the saints] but that of participating in or sharing the needs of the saints. . . . The meaning, therefore, would be that we are to identify ourselves with the needs of the saints and make them our own.[1]

Charles Hodge, in his commentary on Romans, adopted a similar interpretation, saying that we are to regard the needs of the other saints as our own because we are, in fact, members of the same Body.

As John Murray observed, sharing *in* the needs of God's people, making their needs our own, will result in a desire to share *with* them whatever material possessions we have available to help meet those needs. This, of course, was the attitude of those first believers immediately after Pentecost. "No one claimed that any of his possessions was his own, but they shared everything they had" (Acts 4:32).

But the important fact to be noted in Murray's and Hodge's interpretations of Romans 12:13 is that the basis of sharing is *relationship*. It is because we belong to one another and are members of the same Body that we are to make each other's needs our own. If you belong to me, then your needs become my needs and my needs become your needs. Sharing materially with those in need is an experiential outworking of the objective nature of fellowship. It is important to remember that all experiential fellowship is based on an objective relationship. We *are* in fellowship with the other members of the Body; therefore, we should work this out in our daily lives.

Sharing our possessions with other believers in need, then, is an act of obedience to the commands of God and an evidence that we are in the community of believers. This emphasis on sharing as an act of obedience, however, should not cause us to overlook the importance of heartfelt generosity in our giving. God does not intend that we give simply out of grudging obedience, but out of generous and grateful hearts. In 2 Corinthians 9, Paul's classic passage on sharing with others in need, he uses variations of the word "generous" seven different times (verses 5,6,11,13).[2] In fact there is no such thing as grudging obedience. For an action to be truly obedient to God, it must be done from a motivation of genuine love and gratitude to Him.

Generosity is a fruit of the Spirit, but it is also a trait that must be cultivated. One way of cultivating a generous spirit is to gain a greater understanding of and appreciation for our community relationship with other believers. When we truly grasp the fact that we belong to one another, we will want to be generous toward one another, just as parents delight in being generous toward their children.

A joyous experience

Sharing with others in need is meant to be a joyous experience. We have already noted the statement in 2 Corinthians 8:4 in our list of Scripture texts on sharing. In this verse Paul describes how the Macedonian Christians urgently pleaded with him for the privilege of sharing in an offering for the needy saints in Jerusalem. The context indicates that the Macedonians did this with great joy. Paul said, "Out of the most severe trial, their overflowing joy and their extreme poverty welled up in rich generosity" (2 Corinthians 8:2). They obviously enjoyed giving, even in the midst of their poverty.

Solomon spoke of the joy that comes from sharing our possessions with others when he said, "He who refreshes others will himself be refreshed"

(Proverbs 11:25). This joy comes from meeting the needs of God's people, from being obedient to His will, and from experiencing His grace at work in our lives. The very day that I was working on these paragraphs, I learned of a financial need of some Christian friends. What a joy it is to be able to send some of our family's funds to another family who has a critical need at this time. I am already anticipating the joy it will bring to them as they see God supply their needs through other members of the Body.

God is glorified

Sharing with God's people in need also results in thanksgiving and praise to God. Paul indicates in 2 Corinthians 9:11-13 that our generosity toward those in need "will result in thanksgiving to God," and that because of such sharing "men will praise God" for such obedience and generosity.

The Westminster Shorter Catechism states that the chief end of man is to glorify God and enjoy Him forever. Sharing with others glorifies God because other believers in need are looking to Him to meet their needs, and so they receive gifts from us as also from God. The act of sharing on our part is also an act of God. God uses a variety of people and means to accomplish His work. He has promised to supply the needs of His children, and He often does this through others of His children. He has ordained that the members of the Body should care for one another through this means of mutual giving. When we give, we should desire that God receive the credit and thanksgiving. If the recipient of our sharing gives us thanks, that is well and good, but our desire should be that God is glorified.

Consider what a privilege it is to be used in this manner to bring glory to God. Because God is limitless in His resources, He can meet the need of our brother or sister in an infinite number of ways. Whatever way He chooses will bring glory to His name. Our brother in need would be just as grateful to God if he found a $100 bill lying on the sidewalk (in a situation where it was impossible to find the owner) as he would if he received a $100 check from us. But in God's plan for the Body, He more often chooses to receive glory through our acts of obedience and generosity than through impersonal providential circumstances. In this way, not only does God receive glory but also the fellowship among believers is strengthened.

As we give, God's grace is displayed in our lives. Paul makes it very clear in 2 Corinthians 8:1 and 9:14 that the obedience and generosity in sharing is a result of God's grace at work in our lives. We are not naturally inclined to take from our pockets to meet the needs of others. But God's grace can transform us from selfish graspers to generous sharers. And this transforming grace of God at work in us brings glory to Him.

Where to share

So far in this chapter we have discussed primarily our sharing with other believers who are in need. Koinonia is a sharing together in the Body of Christ that results in a sharing what we have with one another. This may seem largely theoretical to some Christians due to the fact that they are personally acquainted with so few fellow believers who have needs. In fact, many Christians worshiping in a typical middle-class church may be hard-pressed to identify a single believer in their midst who has a material need to be met.

However, if we are truly serious about applying this sharing aspect of fellowship, and if we ask God for opportunities to do so and are alert to those opportunities, God will bring them to our attention. A few paragraphs back, I mentioned learning of a financial need of some friends of ours. Because these people are not normally needy, one would not usually think of this particular family as an opportunity to share with God's people who are in need. But a serious medical problem, compounded by other events—as my friend wrote, "When it rains, it pours"—has put a serious strain on this family's finances and provided an opportunity for other members of the Body to share in their need and to help them meet it.

I think of another occasion when I was prompted to take a friend to a men's clothing store to buy him a tweed jacket and slacks. I had no special reason to do this as far as being aware of any need he might have had. I was only responding to an overwhelming awareness of God's generosity to me and a desire to share His blessing with someone else. Only after I told my friend what I wanted to do for him did I learn that on the previous day he had ripped open a sleeve on his only sport jacket and that he was not in a position to buy another one. God brought me the opportunity to share with my friend before I was even aware of his need.

God will do the same for you if you truly want to enter into the fellowship of sharing with others in the Body. As Paul said in 2 Corinthians 9:8, "God is able to make all grace abound to you, so that in all things at all times, having all that you need, you will abound in every good work." God will not only bring to your attention opportunities to share, but He will also provide the means with which you can do it.

God does give us the privilege of directly meeting the material needs of people we know personally, but much of our sharing today may be done through our giving to organizations that specialize in identifying and meeting the material needs of others. There is precedent for this in the New Testament. Paul was something of a one-man "relief agency" as he went to the gentile churches in Macedonia and Achaia presenting the needs of the poor saints back in Jerusalem. In the same manner, a number of evangelical relief agencies today present to us the needs of believers in ghetto areas of our cities or in poverty-stricken areas overseas.

Though our family from time to time has opportunity to help meet the needs of people we know personally, the vast majority of our giving toward the needs of others is done through our church or some of the agencies we have come to know and respect.

Most of these organizations minister to believers *and* unbelievers. But they always minister materially in the name of Christ with the objective that their ministry will eventually result in many of the unbelievers coming to Christ. In our world today, it is impractical, and probably not biblical, to seek to restrict the sharing of our material possessions to believers alone. Paul said we are to "do good to *all* people, especially to those who belong to the family of believers" (Galatians 6:10). While there is a priority of sharing with believers first, we must not neglect the unbeliever. The practical fact is that in most situations of major need today it is impossible to separate the believers from the unbelievers.

Regularity of sharing

One of the principles of giving most often cited in teaching on the subject is that of regular and systematic giving. Paul's instruction to the Corinthian believers, "On the first day of every week, each one of you should set aside a sum of money in keeping with his income" (1 Corinthians 16:2), is the Scripture passage used to support this principle. But Paul's instruction was given in the specific context of a collection for needy Christians in Jerusalem. Therefore, our giving to meet the needs of needy believers, and perhaps unbelievers, should be as systematic and regular as our giving to our local church or to mission agencies that we support.

Naturally there will be unexpected needs that come to our attention from time to time, especially if we are seeking to exercise the fellowship of sharing. But the foundation of our giving to meet the needs of others should be a regular systematic program through our local church or through agencies specifically organized and equipped to meet the vast needs in the world today.

In addition to 1 Corinthians 16:1-2, the other passage most often used to teach principles of Christian giving is 2 Corinthians 9:6-8. Yet both of these passages have to do with sharing by the gentile churches with the needy saints among the Jews in Jerusalem. We see, then, that the most basic passages in the New Testament on the subject of Christian giving relate not to giving to our local church, to campus ministry staff members, or even to missionaries overseas, but to the sharing of our material possessions with others in need. Despite the clear setting of these scriptural principles in the context of relieving the distress of other believers, most present-day Christians have lost sight of this important aspect of giving.

We in the Body tend to give to our local churches, to various parachurch ministries at home, and to mission works overseas, but we tend to give very little to other members of the Body in need. The reason for this, I believe, lies in the fact that we have lost sight of the true meaning of fellowship, of the biblical practice of koinonia.

Obviously we should give to our local church as well as to various other ministries both at home and abroad that are doing God's work. My appeal is not to slight those ministries but to balance our giving by including this highly important aspect of fellowship.

In the United States even the tax laws work against our sharing with other believers in need. The government allows us to deduct our gifts to charitable or religious organizations from our taxable income but does not allow us to deduct our gifts to needy individuals. Consequently, many American Christians have fallen into the trap of giving only where they can receive a tax deduction, thus failing to recognize or respond to the needs of individuals. It would be a good spiritual exercise for many of us to deliberately plan to give to some needy individuals without thought of any tax deduction advantage.

In Chapter 5 we saw that God is pleased when His people share with each other on a spiritual basis, even to the point of having a book of remembrance written about it (Malachi 3:16). But God is also pleased when we share with each other on a material level. Hebrews 13:16 says, "Do not forget to do good and to share with others, for with such sacrifices God is pleased." What a privilege we have to glorify God and to please Him through the fellowship of sharing our possessions with those in need.

Because of the tendency of certain people to abuse the grace of sharing, I feel compelled to add a word of warning at the close of this chapter. In my travels to different cities, I have become aware of a class of people who are not needy but rather irresponsible. These people travel from city to city, especially in the more scenic parts of the U.S.A., living off the generosity of churches that are sincerely seeking to apply the fellowship of sharing with people in need. These people apparently have no desire to work or to worship with God's people. They have been known, however, to attend a worship service only for the purpose of being invited to have a meal with a family. To such people who are not only irresponsible but also deceitful, the words of the Apostle Paul apply very aptly: "If a man will not work, he shall not eat" (2 Thessalonians 3:10).

Notes

1. John Murray, *The Epistle to the Romans*, Volume 2 (Grand Rapids: Eerdmans Publishing Co., 1968), page 133.
2. This is true only in the *New International Version.* Other translations use words such as "bountiful" or "liberal" to express the same idea.

9
Supporting Your Local Ministry

ANYONE WHO RECEIVES
INSTRUCTION IN THE WORD
MUST SHARE ALL GOOD
THINGS WITH HIS
INSTRUCTOR.

Galatians 6:6

During a recent Bible-teaching ministry at a church, the chairman of the deacons asked for my ideas on how to determine a fair and adequate salary for their pastor. In the course of our conversation, this deacon made a very perceptive statement that amazed me. He said, "Our pastor is our most valuable asset. He is worth far more than this church building." What a refreshingly different viewpoint from the all-too-common one that puts great emphasis on a church building while neglecting or inadequately seeing to the care of those who make our church buildings valuable.

So very often it seems that we Christians are susceptible to the kind of world John Calvin described: "It is and always has been the world's nature to stuff the stomachs of the ministers of Satan and hardly and grudgingly to supply godly pastors with their necessary food."[1] While "grudgingly" may seem like too strong a word in many instances, neglect or indifference is just as evil both in our attitude and in its practical effect.

We have seen that one of the principal expressions of koinonia is to share what we have with others. This sharing with one another, whether it be on a spiritual or material level, arises out of the most basic meaning of koinonia as a relationship: a sharing together of the common life we have in Christ. Sharing our material possessions with other believers in need is the most frequently mentioned expression of koinonia in the New Testament, as we saw in Chapter 8. Sharing materially with missionaries in a partnership of the gospel is also clearly taught by the Apostle Paul, as we saw in Chapter 6.

Sharing with our teachers

There is yet one more sharing of our material possessions mentioned by Paul: sharing with those who teach us the Word of God. In Galatians 6:6 Paul said, "Anyone who receives instruction in the word must share [*koinōneitō*] all good things with his instructor." That is, those who are taught the Scriptures have a duty to care for the material needs of those who labor in teaching. This is another New Testament expression of fellowship.[2]

Paul envisions a reciprocal relationship of sharing: the teacher sharing spiritual truth and the pupil sharing material possessions. It is the same kind of reciprocity mentioned by Paul when he said, "If the Gentiles have shared in the Jews' spiritual blessings, they owe it to the Jews to share with them their material blessings" (Romans 15:27). He states the same principle in 1 Corinthians 9:11 when he says, "If we have sown spiritual seed among you, is it too much if we reap a material harvest from you?"

Clearly it is the duty of believers who are taught the Word of God by men set apart for that purpose to care for the material needs of those who teach them. Paul is emphatic about this. The *New International Version* translation of Galatians 6:6 says that the pupil "*must* share" with his instructor. Paul is even more emphatic about this principle in 1 Corinthians 9:14 when he says, "In the same way, *the Lord has commanded* that those who preach the gospel should receive their living from the gospel" (italics added). Though Paul is writing as an inspired apostle and thus speaking the very Word of God in his own right, here he appeals on this important issue to the command of the Lord Himself.

But the appeal in Galatians 6:6 for financial support, though stated as an imperative, is based not on law but on love—on the bond of koinonia. The sharing between pupil and instructor is another expression of the relationship they have in Christ. Where this vital relationship of sharing together their common life in Christ is recognized, the appropriate expressions of that relationship will inevitably occur. In the case at hand, it is appropriate for the teacher to share spiritual truth with those who need to be taught, and it is appropriate for those who are taught to share materially with the teacher.

Application for today

In Paul's day there was a much more direct relationship between the teacher and those who were taught. There were no church buildings to maintain, no church programs to fund, and no lengthy church budgets to approve at the annual church business meeting. The only issue was the support of those who worked full-time at preaching and teaching. Apparently there was no stated salary for those men. Their livelihood depended entirely on the believers' understanding of the importance of sharing materially with their teacher.

In our day of diversified church budgets, multiple church staffs, and the existence of many fine parachurch ministers, how is this principle of sharing materially with our teachers to be worked out? How should the typical committed church member seek to apply Galatians 6:6 when he is asked to give to a church budget that includes programs, facilities, administration, and staff? It is our responsibility as church members to see that those whom we have called to work full-time in our churches are fairly and adequately compensated. It does not matter whether the staff person is the teaching pastor, the Christian education director, or the youth minister. The principle that those who preach the gospel should get their living from the gospel still applies.

Very often pastoral salaries are considered

delicate and even confidential matters because it is felt that some church members will think, "The pastor is getting too much." What an indictment of our Christianity! More often than not, the pastor is getting too little. Though pastoral salaries are usually set by church boards, we as individual members still have a responsibility to see that our representatives on those boards establish pastoral salaries that are adequate and that meet Paul's criteria of sharing "all good things" with those who instruct us.

Parachurch ministries

What about the full-time staff of organizations that minister outside the local church, such as military or campus ministries? Paul's instructions would apply to any situation where the "instructor" has been set apart as a full-time teacher or a gospel worker. Those who are taught are to take the initiative to share materially with their teacher. Those who are taught should not wait for the worker to make his needs known. Obviously new believers must be instructed in this area, as in all other areas of the Christian life, but upon receiving this instruction, it is their responsibility to act on it.

There is still another group of full-time laborers in the gospel that we need to consider: those who labor among people who cannot support them. Instances of this sort would be those who minister in our prisons, in the ghettos of our large cities, and even on campuses of suburban high schools. These people should be considered as missionaries, whether they labor at home or overseas, and they should thus be supported on a partnership basis, as we discussed in Chapter 6. God has given the Church the responsibility of evangelizing and discipling not only on the foreign mission field but also in the inner-city areas, in prisons, etc. Obviously none of us can contribute to the support of all the worthy organizations that provide help to the disadvantaged and the forgotten, but we do need to prayerfully consider what God wants us to do.

The Bible teaches that God wants us to share our possessions with others as an expression of fellowship. We have discussed three distinct groups of people with whom we are to share: (1) other believers in need, (2) those who teach us the Word of God, and (3) those who are missionaries, either at home or abroad, with whom we become financial partners in the gospel.

In all these instances it is important for us to realize that we are sharers, not just givers. The distinction between a sharer and a giver is very important. The giver is under no obligation; he gives from a strictly voluntary point of view. The sharer is under an obligation, although it is an obligation of love. It is a responsibility of relationship or partnership. As a giver, I can choose to give or not to give to the United Way, for example, because I am under no obligation. But I cannot choose whether or not to meet the needs of my own children, at least to the extent that I am able. I am under the obligation of our relationship and of love to meet their needs.

It is the same in the Body of Christ. We belong to one another in a relationship of koinonia. That relationship obligates us to fulfill the terms of the relationship: to *share* with other members of the Body, either those personally in need or those involved in gospel work.

So the sharing of our financial resources with others in the Body of Christ is an obligation, but it is an obligation of love, of the relationship of koinonia. Those who truly understand koinonia *want* to share. They accept their responsibility to share with great joy. They are like those Macedonian believers who, in spite of their own extreme poverty, pleaded with Paul for the opportunity of sharing in the offering he was collecting for the poor saints in Jerusalem.

Notes

1. John Calvin, *Calvin's New Testament Commentaries,* Volume 2, translated by T.H.L. Parker (Grand Rapids: Eerdmans Publishing Co., 1965), page 112.
2. The vast majority of commentators and translators accept the meaning of *koinōneitō* in Galatians 6:6 as sharing materially with the teacher. A few interpret it as having spiritual fellowship with the teacher. For a statement of this view, see *Word Studies in the Greek New Testament* by Kenneth S. Wuest. Though I respect Wuest's scholarship, I agree with the majority in this instance.

10
The Fellowship of Suffering

I WANT TO KNOW CHRIST AND THE POWER OF HIS RESURRECTION AND THE FELLOWSHIP OF SHARING IN HIS SUFFERINGS.

Philippians 3:10

We come now to an aspect of fellowship that most of us would probably just as soon pass by: the active desire "to know Christ and the power of his resurrection and the fellowship of sharing in his sufferings" (Philippians 3:10). Most Christians can appreciate Paul's yearning to know Christ in a more intimate way, and we certainly identify with Paul's desire to experience the power of the resurrected Christ in his life. But we pause a bit when we come to his desire to know the fellowship of sharing in His sufferings.

Suffering for Christ

None of us enjoys suffering or seeks it out just for its own sake. Paul was no exception to this legitimate human instinct. But there were two strong factors at work in Paul to make him desire the fellowship of sharing in Christ's sufferings. First, it meant the privilege of sharing in *Christ's* sufferings, that is, suffering for the sake of Christ. Paul desired to share with Christ in His sufferings since he would thereby advance the cause of Christ and build up His Church. Writing to another body of believers, the Apostle Paul said, "Now I rejoice in what was suffered for you, and I fill up in my flesh what is still lacking in regard to Christ's afflictions, for the sake of his body, which is the church" (Colossians 1:24). Paul knew that, at least in the day in which he lived, identification with Christ and, in particular, labor on behalf of Christ inevitably resulted in suffering. But he was prepared for that suffering. Indeed, he welcomed it and rejoiced in it, since by that means he could extend Christ's Kingdom and build up His Church.

How different was Paul's attitude from the typical twentieth-century middle-class Christian attitude of today. We have somehow gotten the idea that the abundant life Jesus promised in John 10:10 means an abundance of health, wealth, and happiness. The idea of suffering for the sake of Christ is foreign to us. We have substituted the pursuit of happiness for the pursuit of holiness. We hesitate to sacrifice even our material possessions for His cause, let alone sacrificing our lives or the lives of our children upon the altar of His service.

But over and over again in the New Testament the path to glory with Christ is indicated to be the path of suffering with Him and for Him. Here are just two of many examples from Scripture that emphasize the importance of the path of suffering. Paul said, "Now if we are children, then we are heirs—heirs of God and co-heirs with Christ, if indeed we share in his sufferings in order that we may also share in his glory" (Romans 8:17). And Peter said, "Rejoice that you participate in the sufferings of Christ, so that you may be overjoyed when his glory is revealed" (1 Peter 4:13). If we desire to experience the totality of fellowship with Christ, we must expect to experience the fellowship of His sufferings.

Communion in suffering

This brings us to the second factor at work within Paul to cause him to desire to share in Christ's sufferings: the prospect of fellowship or communion with Christ in His sufferings. The Lord Jesus Christ does not leave His people to suffer alone. The universal testimony of those who have suffered for the sake of Christ and His Church is that they have experienced a deep fellowship, an intimate communion with Him in the midst of their sufferings.

It is difficult for many of us in the Western world to understand or appreciate the fellowship with Christ that comes through suffering for His sake. Few of us have experienced to any significant degree suffering for the cause of Christ, but we should realize that our experience is the exception, not only in the history of the Church but even in our own century. It is commonly reported that more people have been martyred for the cause of Christ in this century than at any other time in history.

But what is the testimony of those who have suffered for the sake of Christ in our own day and throughout Church history? Is it not that they have experienced the presence and love of Christ in a unique way in the midst of their sufferings? These persecuted brothers and sisters of ours can identify with Paul in his desire to experience the fellowship of sharing in Christ's sufferings. They have tasted that Christ is faithful, that nothing can separate them from His love, and that His grace is sufficient for their weaknesses.

We do not, however, need to go into lands of atheistic governments or oppressive religious cultures to find believers suffering for the sake of Christ. Even in our own Western nations many believers experience varying degrees of harassment or persecution at their jobs or even within their own homes. In fact many observers believe that the reason we in the West do not suffer more persecution is because we have accommodated ourselves too much to the world around us. Jesus said to His disciples, "In this world you will have trouble," and, "I have chosen you out of the world. That is why the world hates you" (John 16:33, 15:19). The lifestyle philosophy of living "in the world but not of the world" will ultimately lead to suffering in some form: social rejection, loss of job promotion opportunities (or even the job itself), and misunderstanding from family and friends.

Not everyone, though, who suffers because of his witness for Christ or his stand for Him on the job or in the home experiences the fellowship with Christ that Paul desired and experienced. To experience His fellowship in suffering we must do as the apostles did, rejoicing because we have been counted worthy to suffer for His name (see Acts 5:41). I think of a few instances in my own Christian experience when I suffered to some degree for Christ's sake but did not experience the fellowship of His suffering. I failed to experience this fellowship because of my own reaction to the situation. Instead of rejoicing as the apostles did, I allowed anger, hurt, and resentment to control my thoughts. Instead of seeking comfort and encouragement in fellowship with the Savior and in the privilege of suffering for His sake, I allowed myself to be afflicted with self-pity.

Another reason why some people do not experience the fellowship of Christ in their sufferings is because their sufferings are due not to the offense of the gospel itself but to their own lack of wisdom and gentleness in sharing Christ. Peter said we are to "give the reason for the hope that [we] have . . . with gentleness and respect" (1 Peter 3:15-16). The gospel itself does offend, but we should be sure that it is that gospel message rather than our attitude that is offensive to unbelievers. If when we share Christ in an overbearing or argumentative manner we experience hostility and rejection, we will not experience the fellowship of His sufferings. Such rejection is not suffering for His sake but for our own mishandling of the gospel in our manner of presenting it. Those who experience rejection should honestly seek to determine if it is because of their own attitude or truly because of the offense of the Cross. If they are then satisfied that their suffering is indeed for Christ, not for their presentation of Christ, then they should seek comfort and encouragement from Him in the fellowship of His sufferings and rejoice that they have been given the privilege of suffering for Him.

But even when we have offered ourselves as living sacrifices on the altar of His service and have experienced to some small degree rejection and suffering for His sake, the fact still remains that most of us in the Western world know little of what it means to share in the fellowship of His sufferings. Is there anything, then, in this aspect of fellowship that is truly applicable to us, or is this just one part of New Testament fellowship that most of us will never experience to any significant degree? Well, there are other ways through which we can enter into the fellowship of Christ's sufferings that should be the experience of all Christians everywhere.

Suffering with other believers

As Saul of Tarsus was on his way to Damascus to persecute the believers in that city, he was confronted by the risen Christ. He heard the voice of Jesus saying, "Saul, Saul, why do you persecute me?" In answer to Saul's question, "Who are you, Lord?" Jesus replied, "I am Jesus, whom you are persecuting" (Acts 9:4-5). Now the record is distinctly clear that Saul had already been persecuting the Lord's disciples and that he was on his way at that moment to persecute them again in Damascus. Yet Jesus asked Saul, "Why do you persecute me?" Jesus so closely identified with His people that persecution of them was essentially persecution of Jesus Himself, even though He was then seated at the right hand of His Father. This is a profound truth, one that we do well to ponder in times of trial ourselves. We are so intimately united with Christ that what affects us affects Him.

Now since Christ regards the suffering of believers as His suffering, it follows that we can share in the fellowship of *His* sufferings as we identify with other believers who suffer. The writer of Hebrews said to his readers, "Sometimes you were publicly exposed to insult and persecution; at other times you stood side by side with those who were so treated" (Hebrews 10:33). The phrase "stood side by side with" is the NIV translation of the Greek word *koinōnoi*, meaning literally "companions" or "partners." The writer of Hebrews was saying that his readers had identified with other suffering believers so closely that they stood side by side with them as partners in their sufferings. They literally had *fellowship* with them in their sufferings. Through this relationship they shared in the fellowship of Christ's sufferings.

Once again we are faced with the fact that our contemporary view of fellowship, which usually includes only Christian social activity or perhaps sharing the Word of God together, fails to do justice to the biblical practice of koinonia. Fellowship is much, much more than food and fun, or even more than an enjoyable time over the Scriptures with another believer. Fellowship at times may involve blood, sweat, and tears as we stand side by side with our persecuted brothers and sisters.

Paul said in 1 Corinthians 12 that if one part of the Body suffers, every other part suffers with it. We are to so identify with other members of the Body of Christ that we enter into their sufferings as well as their joys. Those of us who are parents tend to so identify with our children that their hurts become our hurts. Often we feel that we would rather experience pain ourselves instead of having to watch our children suffer because we so identify with them. This feeling is a natural response to the fact that they are a part of us.

Now Paul would say that this identity with the hurts and pains of others should be just as true in the Body of Christ as it is in our family relationships. In fact, he said it should be just as strong as is the empathy among the various parts of the physical body. If one part suffers, every other part suffers with it.

Remember that in Chapter 4 we learned that fellowship is first of all an objective fact denoting a community in Christ of all believers throughout the world. We and those suffering believers in other parts of the world are members of one organism: Christ's Body. And Paul has told us that the different parts of the Body should have equal concern for one another.

Our concern for other members of the Body

of Christ who are suffering should arise from the motive of love. Paul said in Romans 12:10 that we are to "be devoted to one another in brotherly love." That is, because we are all family members, we should express the same quality of love for one another that the members of a devoted, warm-hearted human family show for each other. In fact, our love within the family of God should go far beyond the love of the physical family. John suggests to us in 1 John 3:17 that the love we are to express within the Body is actually the love of God abiding in us. God's love always transcends human love, even human family love, in its ability to reach out to those in need. As we abide in Christ, looking to Him to enable us to love, He will give us the capacity to reach out to fellow members of His Body, even to those we have never met.

Perhaps this thought of reaching out in love to suffering members of the Body whom we have never met seems too idealistic. However, the Bible is a book of idealism on a strictly human plane. None of its commands can be carried out apart from the enabling work of the Holy Spirit. Consider the command, "Husbands, love your wives, just as Christ loved the church and gave himself up for her" (Ephesians 5:25). What man can possibly love his wife, however wonderful she may be, *as Christ loved the Church?* Yet this is the Bible's ideal for us. And by the same token, it is the Bible's ideal for us to love all the other members of the Body with a brotherly love, a love that is expressive of a close family relationship.

Because the Body of Christ is to be found

among all nations, those of us in countries where there is no persecution have the opportunity to share in the fellowship of Christ's sufferings by identifying with our brothers and sisters in countries where persecution does exist. We learned in Chapter 8 that we are to make the material needs of others in the Body our own needs and that, as a consequence, we should seek to help meet those needs. In the same manner, we should so identify with our suffering brothers and sisters that their suffering becomes our suffering, thus moving us to do what we can to relieve that suffering.

The first way we can respond to their suffering is through *fervent prayer* for them, asking God to intervene in their persecutions, or else to grant them a special measure of His grace to endure them. Note, however, that our prayers must be heartfelt and fervent. This is no place for perfunctory, routine praying. Think again of the parent-child relationship. When a child is hurting, the Christian parent does not engage in perfunctory prayer for divine relief. Rather, his prayers are intense and urgent. It is not a matter of indifference whether or not God answers those prayers. The genuine empathy and concern for the suffering child that grows out of the parent-child relationship demands an earnestness in the prayers of the parent for God's intervention.

It should be the same in the Body of Christ. The reason we don't experience this family-like empathy with our suffering brothers and sisters in Christ is that we have not yet been fully gripped by the truth that we are in a community relationship with them. Even though we may become aware of this basic meaning of fellowship, the knowledge of the truth does not so grip us that it changes our lives. It may be argued that this view of the Body of Christ is an idealistic and unattainable view. The question we should address, however, is whether it is the biblical view. Does God intend that we so closely identify with our suffering brothers and sisters that their hurts become our hurts? Scripture passages such as Romans 12:15, 1 Corinthians 12:25-26, and Hebrews 10:33-34 would indicate that the answer is yes.

There is an example from the life of the Apostle Paul that will help us appreciate the idealism of Scripture and the fact that that idealism is to be our own goal. In Colossians 1:29-2:1, Paul twice used the word "struggling" to describe his ministry. He said he was struggling to present everyone perfect in Christ but that he was also struggling for the believers at Colosse and Laodicea, and *for all who had not met him personally*. We have already seen that the word translated "struggling" literally means "agonizing." It is a verb of very great intensity.

We are not too surprised to learn that Paul agonized in his direct labors to present everyone perfect in Christ. After all, he was an intense man by personality even before his conversion, and he was obviously totally committed to his ministry. But how could he struggle for those he had never even met? The obvious answer is by prayer. Paul prayed with the same intensity for believers he had never met as he prayed for and labored to present the gospel to those he did meet. It is possible to pray with fervent intensity, even to agonize, for believers we have never met. Granted, this is the ideal. But we must pray and work for the ideal, for it was Jesus who said, "Be perfect, therefore, as your heavenly Father is perfect" (Matthew 5:48).

This does not mean that we have a responsibility to pray for every single suffering believer in the world with the intensity of which Paul speaks. It does suggest that we have a responsibility to pray for some, either individually or as groups—the suffering believers in the Soviet Union, for example. It is our duty to be sensitive to God's leading as to which suffering believers we are to identify with. After we have determined where our responsibility lies, we should then enter into the fellowship of their suffering.

Often we have opportunity to do more than pray. Sometimes it is possible to do something tangible toward relieving the plight of our suffering brothers and sisters in Christ. Our family, for example, has given through one mission agency to provide financial aid to the families of believers who have been imprisoned for the gospel. As we pray for the suffering believers, we can also ask God to show us what we can do toward meeting their needs.

Another way we may be able to assist suffering Christians is through our government. At times our government, in response to a few caring Christians, has exerted sufficient influence on a persecuting foreign government to somewhat relieve the pressure on suffering believers abroad. It is likely that much more would be done if more of us were truly concerned and expressed this concern to our government leaders.

Suffering over sin

A third way by which we may enter into the fellowship of Christ's sufferings is through our resolute response to sin wherever we find it, whether in ourselves or in society around us. Genesis 6:6 says that because of man's sin, "The LORD was grieved that he had made man on the earth, and his heart was filled with pain." Most of the time we view sin in terms of its effects on us, or our family, or friends, or perhaps on the society around us. We seldom think of sin in terms of its effect on God. But sin sorely grieves the heart of God. Sin is a rejection of His law and a rebellion against His authority, bringing alienation between God and man.

Take, for example, the problem of abortion. We tend to view this practice as a crime against society, as the legalized killing of millions of unborn children. Our concern focuses on the injustice toward those babies and the dehumanizing effect on society as a whole. But is it not God's heart that is most grieved and filled with pain over this crime? Is it not His law that is broken and the children created in His image that are killed?

Missionary statesman Bob Pierce prayed, "God break my heart with the things that break your heart." Pierce saw the physical suffering of vast multitudes in war-ravaged or famine-stricken countries. And what do *we* see? What is the state of our hearts as we view the sin that is so rampant in our society today? If Christ grieved over unrepentant Jerusalem, does He not grieve over unrepentant America as well? If we would fully enter into the fellowship of His sufferings, we must begin to see sin from His point of view.

How do we view our own sin? Too often we see it in terms of its effect on ourselves. We are irritated with our lack of self-control in succumbing to some besetting sin, or we are disappointed with ourselves over our failure to withstand some temptation, or we are ashamed that we have failed to do what we should have done. Our response in all of these situations is basically inward and self-centered. As we begin to see our sin from God's point of view, however, we will begin to grieve over it as He grieves over it. And as we join in His grief, we will also in this small way enter into the fellowship of His sufferings.

11 The Fellowship of Serving

YOU . . . WERE CALLED TO BE FREE. BUT DO NOT USE YOUR FREEDOM TO INDULGE THE SINFUL NATURE; RATHER, SERVE ONE ANOTHER IN LOVE.

Galatians 5:13

During his visit to Taiwan, Dawson Trotman hiked with a Taiwanese pastor back into some of the mountain villages to minister the Word of God to the national Christians. Because the roads and trails were wet, they returned home wet and cold, their shoes covered with mud. Much later, someone asked this Taiwanese pastor what he remembered most about Dawson Trotman. Without hesitation the man replied, "He cleaned my shoes."

When Trotman and the pastor returned that afternoon, as the custom was, they removed their shoes at the doorway. The pastor went on into the kitchen to prepare some tea. How surprised he was when he returned in a few minutes to see Trotman sitting on the floor with a small stick, a piece of cloth, and some water, cleaning his shoes. Such a spirit of servanthood marked Dawson Trotman throughout his Christian life. He died as he lived, actually giving his life to rescue someone else from drowning.

The concept of servanthood is basic to the biblical practice of koinonia. Fellowship involves sharing what we have with others. One of the most valuable things we can share is ourselves: our time, our talents, and our energies in serving one another in the Body of Christ. Dawson Trotman was a master at spiritual fellowship, but he also knew how to share himself in serving others.

The greatest model and teacher of servanthood was of course the Lord Jesus Christ. Paul said of Him that He took "the very nature of a servant" (Philippians 2:7), and Jesus said of Himself that "the Son of Man did not come to be served, but to serve, and to give his life as a ransom for many" (Matthew 20:28).

Although Jesus' entire life was one of service, the most notable example of His servanthood was that of washing His disciples' feet on the evening of His betrayal, recorded for us in John 13:1-17. This instance was notable both because of the setting and because of the mundane nature of His service.

Jesus knew that it was the night of His betrayal and that the very next morning He would suffer on a cross for the sins of the world. He would, from our viewpoint, have had every reason to be preoccupied with His imminent sufferings. Yet Jesus took time to tend to a duty—washing the feet of guests—that was usually left to the lowest servant in a household. He did this with full awareness of His own divine dignity. John says of Him, "Jesus knew that the Father had put all things under his power, and that he had come from God and was returning to God; so he got up from the meal, took off his outer clothing, and wrapped a towel around his waist . . . and began to wash his disciples' feet."

It was not in spite of His greatness but *because* of His greatness that Jesus served His disciples on that evening. Through His own attitude toward servanthood, He taught us that true greatness in the Kingdom of God consists not in position or authority but in serving one another. If we are to master the scriptural principles of true biblical fellowship, we must master this one: True greatness in the Kingdom of Heaven consists in serving one another. Jesus said, "Whoever wants to become great among you must be your servant" (Matthew 20:26).

Jesus knew that the Father had put all things under His power. Jesus also recognized that He Himself was the sovereign God, that He was both Creator and Sustainer of the universe. His Incarnation and humiliation did not in any way alter the fact that He was the eternal God the Son. And in full knowledge of who He was and the authority that was His, Jesus arose from the table and began to wash the feet of the disciples. In the mind of Jesus, acts of mundane service were not inconsistent with authority and greatness, but rather an integral part of it.

Jesus' concept of greatness—and obviously His is the correct one—is so contrary to the world's sense of values that even we Christians have difficulty grasping it. Even the disciples vied among themselves for rank and position rather than for the privilege of serving one another. The mother of James and John asked Jesus that her two sons might sit at His right hand and at His left hand in His Kingdom. And on that memorable evening of the Last Supper, the disciples were still disputing among themselves who was greatest. Their action may seem presumptuous to us today, but essentially we are not much different. Our actions may be more subtle and refined, but too often our attitude is one of striving for position and recognition rather than striving for the privilege of serving one another.

We have observed earlier in this book that competition has no place in the fellowship of believers. Rather, we are to honor one another above ourselves. Serving one another within the Body is a very practical and concrete way to honor one another. By serving I simply mean *doing* helpful deeds for one another. Jesus washed His disciples' feet. Dawson Trotman cleaned a national pastor's shoes. Paul, shipwrecked on the island of Malta, gathered a pile of brushwood to put on the fire built for his fellow passengers. Each one of these acts was incredibly simple and mundane in and of itself. But this is what servanthood within the fellowship of believers is all about: being alert to the little things that need to be done, and then doing them.

Characteristics of a servant

One of the beauties of servanthood is that it requires no special talent or spiritual gifts. Of course, as we saw in Chapter 7, we are to use our spiritual gifts to serve one another. And if God has given us certain natural abilities, we also want to be good stewards of those abilities by serving others in the Body. But it requires no spiritual gift or talent to wash feet, clean shoes, or gather firewood. All that is required is a servant's attitude.

A well-known Bible teacher once spoke to a men's group at a church in the Washington, D.C., area. Afterward he noticed a man who stayed behind to remove and stack the chairs. Upon inquiring he learned that the man stacking the chairs was a busy United States Senator. It did not take the talent or ability of a senator to stack chairs. But it did take the attitude of a servant.

No one ever gets to a place within society as a whole or within the Body of Christ in particular where he or she is too important to serve others in the ordinary tasks of life. In fact, one of the chief characteristics of a servant is that he serves *downward,* that is, to those who by the world's standards are beneath him in position or station in life. It is relatively easy to serve those above us. Even the world expects this. But Jesus served downward. In addition to His deity, He was, on a strictly human plane, the leader of that band of twelve disciples. He could have asked one of them to wash all their feet, but He chose to do it Himself.

Jesus recognized that in the world the lesser

serves the greater. At one time He said, "Who is greater, the one who is at the table or the one who serves? Is it not the one who is at the table? But I am among you as one who serves" (Luke 22:27). But although it may be true in the world that the lesser serves the greater, in the Body of Christ it is to be different. Again Jesus said, "I have set you an example [in serving] that you should do as I have done for you" (John 13:15).

Solomon's son, King Rehoboam, did not learn the lesson of serving downward. Shortly after ascending the throne of Israel, he was approached by some of the people who asked him that the heavy yoke of taxation and forced labor be lightened. Upon consulting the elders who had advised his father, Rehoboam was told, "If today you will be a servant to these people and serve them and give them a favorable answer, they will always be your servants" (1 Kings 12:7). Rehoboam, however, did not listen; he did not choose to serve downward. As a result, he lost ten of the twelve tribes from his kingdom and created an irreparable separation within the nation of God's people.

Recently I learned of the owner of a large and successful automobile dealership who has learned to serve downward. When asked on a radio interview about his number-one priority in running his business, he answered, "To serve my employees." What a surprising answer! I would not have been surprised if he had answered, "To serve my customers." Almost everyone would say that. After all, that is the way to maximize profits and, besides, it sounds very noble, or pious if one happens to be a Christian. But this man runs his business to serve his employees. He believes that his first priority is to provide for his employees a decent and fair place to work and earn their livelihood. He has learned to serve downward.

As I study the subject of servanthood in the Bible, I am struck by the number of instances where the servant was in a position, from the world's point of view, above those he served. Paul, for example, said, "You yourselves know that these hands of mine have supplied my own needs *and the needs of my companions*" (Acts 20:34, italics added). We would expect Paul's companions, who happened to be those he was training in the ministry, to care for his needs. But Paul was a servant. He supplied their needs.

Serving others usually requires no special talent or ability. But it does take a servant attitude to want to serve others, as well as an observant eye and mind to see what needs to be done. If we have a servant attitude, we can develop an observant eye. The reason most of us do not see opportunities to serve is that we are continually thinking about ourselves instead of others. We have not learned that we are to look not only to our own interests but also to the interests of others.

Of course, God must give us a servant attitude. We cannot change our own hearts. But we can allow God to change us through our Bible study, prayer, and obedience. We need to fill our minds with Scriptures that teach servanthood, many of them cited in this chapter. We must also pray earnestly for God to give us the heart of a servant. And then we must obey, responding to every opportunity to serve that He places before us. If we want God to give us a servant's heart, we cannot pick and choose our occasions of serving others. He changes us only as we demonstrate consistent obedience.

As important as it is to serve downward, however, we must not think of such acts of submissiveness as the only opportunity to serve one another. Most of us find ourselves in positions, even within the Body of Christ, where we are under the authority or supervision of another. The Sunday school teacher reports to his or her superintendent, the missionary reports to his field director, and the choir member is under the authority of the choir director, at least for a limited time. Some of these situations are voluntary while others, as in the case of the missionary, are vocational assignments. In either case, however, the common denominator is carrying out the instructions or directions of someone over us.

As we serve those whom God has placed over us in the Body of Christ, the most important character trait is that of faithfulness or trustworthiness. Can the person over us count on us to do the job we have been given to do? Or will we, because of a lack of commitment to the task, fail to fulfill our responsibility? Few things are more distressing to a person in a position of responsibility for the work of others than to not be able to count on those people to do their job. As Solomon observed in such a picturesque fashion, "Like a bad tooth or a lame foot is reliance on the unfaithful in times of trouble" (Proverbs 25:19). My observation after years of serving in both a Christian organization and a local church is that the lack of a serious commitment to faithfulness in assigned or agreed-on tasks is a major problem among Christians. We somehow feel that if we are serving in a voluntary capacity, commitment to faithfulness is not important. But God is the one who requires that we be faithful.

Writing under the inspiration of the Spirit of God, Paul said, "Now it is required that those who have been given a trust must prove faithful" (1 Corinthians 4:2). And Jesus said, "If you have not been trustworthy with someone else's property [or responsibility], who will give you property of your own?" (Luke 16:12). Whether our responsibilities to serve have been given to us directly by God or through someone over us in our church or Christian organization does not matter. In either case God requires that we be faithful in carrying out our assigned or accepted responsibilities.

Challenges of a servant

It is not easy to be a servant to others in the Body of Christ, regardless of whether we are serving upward or downward, or simply serving our neighbor or friend. As someone once observed, the true test of whether we are a servant is that we don't mind being treated like one.

In Luke 17:7-10 Jesus describes the challenges facing those who have put themselves in the position to be servants.

> "Suppose one of you had a servant plowing or looking after the sheep. Would he say to the servant when he comes in from the field, 'Come along now and sit down to eat'? Would he not rather say, 'Prepare my supper, get yourself ready and wait on me while I eat and drink; after that you may eat and drink'? Would he thank the servant because he did what he was told to do? So you also, when you have done everything you were told to do, should say, 'We are unworthy servants; we have only done our duty.'"

Such an attitude toward a servant may sound heartless and perhaps even cruel to us today, but apparently it was a typical attitude in the days of Jesus. Unfortunately, some of this attitude exists within the Body of Christ today—not deliberately, perhaps, but nevertheless just as real and challenging to those who would be servants.

Observe the *inconsiderateness* of the master in verses 7-8. The servant has worked all day and is obviously tired and hungry. Yet before he can rest and eat, he must prepare and serve the master's meal. A lack of consideration toward those serving is too often evident within the Body. Many Christians are self-centered. They are thoughtless and impatient. They make demands and create extra work for others. They don't clean up after themselves when they have a class party in the church social room. They fail to plan ahead, and then they need something done "right now."

Mothers, even in Christian homes, are typical

victims of the inconsiderateness of others. The athletic uniform, dropped in the bedroom three days ago, suddenly needs to be washed immediately. Dad is late for dinner and doesn't call. Toys, games, and various articles of clothing are scattered around the house for Mom to pick up. Never mind how it *should* be; this is too often the way it *is*. Mom is a servant, and the rest of the family members are often inconsiderate.

We tend to resent the inconsiderate actions of others, but if we want to be true servants we must learn to bear with them. Quite apart from what a child or husband or Sunday school class needs to learn about being considerate, if we are to be servants within the Body, we must learn to accept the inconsiderateness of others.

Then observe the *ingratitude* of the master whom Jesus described. "Would he thank the servant because he did what he was told to do?" Jesus asked. Suppose the athletic uniform is washed on time and the dinner is kept hot, waiting for Dad's late arrival. All the miscellaneous items dropped around the house are picked up and put in their proper place. Does Mom get thanked? Too often she does not. After all, that's what Moms are supposed to do.

How about the Sunday school teacher who shows up with a well-prepared lesson Sunday after Sunday. Does anyone ever think to thank her for her faithful service? Or consider the person who works many hours behind the scenes to handle the administrative and logistical details for a weekend retreat or conference. How seldom is that person's labor adequately acknowledged. Yes, if we are to accept the challenge of being a servant, we must be prepared to accept ingratitude, to accept being taken for granted by thoughtless members of the Body.

But Jesus does not stop with our acceptance of inconsiderateness and ingratitude. He presses home the role of a servant even more. When we have done our job as a servant and have borne up under inconsiderateness and ingratitude, we are not to congratulate ourselves for our heroic role. Rather, we are to humbly say, "We are unworthy servants; we have only done our duty."

If we aspire to be servants, we must accept the role of a servant. This is the toughest of all the demands of servanthood. We must accept the fact that God, in calling us to be servants, wants us to accept inconsiderateness and ingratitude as part of our lives. After we have endured the inconsiderateness and overlooked the ingratitude, we are simply to say, "I have only done my duty; I have only done what God has called me to do."

Quite obviously I have painted a rather dark picture of the Body of Christ in its treatment of servants. Happily, considerateness and gratitude are shown much of the time. The fact is that all of us are constantly changing roles from serving to being served. When we are being served, we need to be sensitive to the demands we make and careful to express gratitude when someone else serves us. But when we are serving, we need to accept our role and serve as unto the Lord, whether or not considerateness and gratitude are shown.

The reward of servanthood

One of the most intriguing verses in all the Bible to me is Luke 12:37. In that passage Jesus says, "It will be good for those servants whose master finds them watching when he comes. I tell you the truth, he will dress himself to serve, will have them recline at the table and will come and wait on them."

The context of this verse is the return of the Son of God for His own (see verse 40). Jesus appears to be telling us that in some way He will serve His faithful servants when He comes. As New Testament commentator William Hendriksen said, "What is promised here, therefore, is that our Lord, at his second coming, will, in a manner consonant with his glory and majesty, 'wait on' his faithful servants!"[1]

It is obvious, then, that the servant spirit of Jesus did not exist only during His time as a suffering servant on earth. At His Second Coming He will serve us. The infinitely Greater One will serve the lesser ones. Servanthood is part of the eternal character of God. The reward of servanthood is to be like our Master for all eternity.

Notes

1. William Hendriksen, *Exposition of the Gospel According to Luke* (Grand Rapids: Baker Book House, 1978), page 677.

12
Social Fellowship

HERE I AM! I STAND AT THE DOOR AND KNOCK. IF ANYONE HEARS MY VOICE AND OPENS THE DOOR, I WILL GO IN AND EAT WITH HIM, AND HE WITH ME.

Revelation 3:20

One of the elders at our church said one evening, "We need to get together as a church and just have some fun." He was right. I heartily agreed with him. Our congregation had been through some difficult, stressful times. It is very easy during such hard times to begin to view the Christian life as rather weighty and grim. We needed an occasion to simply enjoy social time together and have some fun.

On numerous occasions throughout these studies I have stated that New Testament fellowship is far more than just Christian social activity. One could get the impression that I am against such activities and that I believe fun or social activities in a Christian context to be sub-spiritual.

This is not the case. Fellowship certainly includes social activity, but the thrust of this book is that it includes *much more.*

In the era in which the New Testament was written, the word *koinōnia* was sometimes used to describe ordinary social interaction among people. The New Testament writers took this word, as they did other Greek words, and gave it a significant spiritual dimension. The objective of this book has been to explore the various facets of that spiritual dimension and, through that broadening, to help us practice fellowship in the rich, full-orbed way that it was practiced in the first-century Church. Sometimes it is necessary to deal with some misconceptions before we can get to the real truth. In this context you can understand my frequent references to the fact that fellowship is *more* than social activity.

God did create men and women to be social creatures, to enjoy relationships with family and friends. We all recognize that the hermit is the rare exception. We feel sorry for the loner, whether on the job, in church, or at school. God created us to enjoy life, to engage in recreation, to have great fun. The old adage, "All work and no play makes Jack a dull boy," is an accepted truism. We need relaxation, fun, and the purely social aspects of Christian fellowship.

The problem has been that Christians often never get beyond the social dimension of fellowship. Thus we need a balanced emphasis on the Church as a caring community, as a partnership in the gospel, and as a Body of believers who mutually build up one another spiritually and share with one another materially.

The Church that was formed on the day of Pentecost demonstrated a balanced approach to fellowship. The people devoted themselves not only to the teaching of the apostles, to prayer, and to fellowship but also to the breaking of bread (Acts 2:42). It is not clear from the text whether the breaking of bread included the observance of the Lord's Supper, but it is clear that it included the sharing together of social meals. Acts 2:46-47 states, "They broke bread in their homes and ate together with glad and sincere hearts, praising God and enjoying the favor of all the people." Those first-century Christians enjoyed social activities together, but they did so in the much larger context of full-orbed New Testament fellowship.

The Lord Jesus Himself is the divine example of participation in Christian social activities. The four Gospels record numerous occasions of His eating in someone's home and of His attendance at feasts and weddings. He performed His first miracle at a wedding celebration in Cana. One of His most moving parables, that of the return of the prodigal son, reaches its climax with the father exclaiming with joy, "Let's have a feast and celebrate" (Luke 15:23). Jesus said of Himself that the Son of Man came eating and drinking, and that because of this participation He was called a glutton and a drunkard (Luke 7:34). While that charge was obviously untrue, it does indicate His reputation as one who thoroughly enjoyed social occasions. By His frequent and hearty participation,

He forever stamped God's approval on Christian social activity. But He also demonstrated what it was meant to be.

Like every other activity in the Christian life, social interaction should have as its ultimate objective the glory of God. "Whether you eat or drink or whatever you do, do it all for the glory of God" (1 Corinthians 10:31). Keeping in mind this objective will help us plan our social activities in such a way that they contribute to the overall New Testament concept of fellowship.

In many of our Christian social activities it is both appropriate and beneficial to turn the thoughts of those who are participating to spiritual values. Whatever form this spiritual dimension may take, whether informal testimonies and sharing or a preplanned "devotional," there should be some natural and obvious correlation between the social and the spiritual aspects of the event. For example, a college campus ministry's Christmas party might have a spiritual theme relating to the First Coming of Christ in which the minds and hearts of those present would be directed toward worship and thanksgiving to God for the indescribable gift of His Son. A Sunday school Fourth of July picnic might close with a time of gathering together to thank God for the freedom He has so graciously given us as a nation and for the spiritual freedom we have in Christ.

Jesus always seemed to use social occasions to evangelize, to heal, or to teach principles of the Christian life. He did these things in such a way that they never seemed artificial or out of place.

For Him, they were always a spontaneous response to the situation at hand.

While we may not have Jesus' divine insight to act spontaneously without any preplanning, we can seek to organically blend the spiritual dimension into our social activities so that it is not just an artificial add-on. There should be some sense of a natural and dynamic interrelationship between the social and spiritual dimensions of our activities.

Should a Christian social activity, then, always have a "devotional" or other obvious spiritual dimension? The answer is no. It all depends on the activity, as well as the immediate objective of the activity. Although we are to glorify God in all we do, the *way* in which we glorify God differs with the activity. Consider a volleyball game on a Saturday morning, sponsored by a Christian group ministering on a state university campus. What is its objective? Perhaps it is an evangelism tool whereby the Christian students can relate to nonChristians in a non-threatening, friendship-building atmosphere. Since the objective is to develop friendships with nonChristians, it is probably not the wisest thing to "have a devotional."

What about the weekly or monthly coffee fellowship in the church basement or the fellowship hall? It is my conviction that this is not a time for idle chitchat about sports, recipes, and the weather. This is a time to deepen acquaintances into friendships and perhaps pave the way for the kind of spiritual fellowship discussed in Chapter 5. I once approached a fellow church member at a coffee fellowship and asked how things had been going for him at his job. As we talked on, I said, "What has the Lord been teaching you lately?" He looked at me, somewhat surprised, and said, "No one's ever asked me that before." He was genuinely touched that someone would take an interest in his spiritual life. Here was an opportunity to get beyond the social into the spiritual dimension of fellowship.

The opportunity to get acquainted with visitors is another excellent use of these coffee fellowship times. For years our church has been known as a friendly church. The coffee fellowship time provides a simple but effective means of expressing that friendliness of our congregation in a warm, congenial atmosphere.

The social dimension of fellowship provides an entrance into the spiritual dimension. We can think of the various levels of fellowship as being represented by a series of concentric circles. The center of this series of circles represents the true you, yourself as you really are. The next outward circle represents your "bosom friend," that person with whom you are so personally and spiritually intimate that you can share everything. The next circle represents those few other believers with whom you have a fairly deep communion or spiritual fellowship, the type described in Chapter 5. The next level represents those Christians in your church or campus discipleship group with whom you have a group relationship. This relationship is a mixture of social and spiritual activities. It is this last circle that is the subject of this chapter.

The lesson to learn from the following illustration is that in developing true spiritual fellowship, we should always start at the outer circle and work inward.

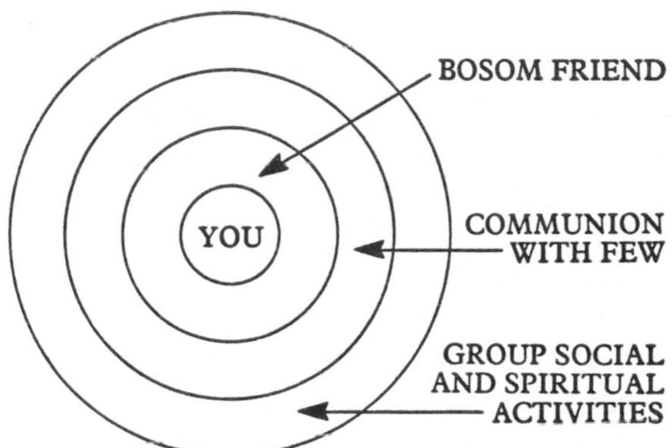

We cannot develop a spiritual intimacy with another believer until we have first had communion or spiritual fellowship with him. And we cannot develop a communion until we have first developed a social relationship. The social dimension, then, always provides the larger context in which spiritual fellowship and one-to-one intimacy are developed.

Consider the instance I have referred to in which I asked that fellow Christian at church, "What has the Lord been teaching you lately?" Such a question would be highly presumptuous and probably offensive if there had not been a significant period of time during which we had first developed a social relationship. My question was an attempt to test the waters to see if I had, over time, earned the right to move into his next circle of spiritual fellowship.

I am not suggesting that, as you move among many believers in this outer circle of group fellowship and social activity, you should be seeking to move to the next inner circle with every Christian you meet. No one has the capacity for an infinite number of deep spiritual relationships. What I am saying is that with those few people with whom you do develop a level of spiritual fellowship, you must begin at the outer circle and earn the right in that level of fellowship to move to the next level.

Thus the social aspect of fellowship is important. It does need to be kept in balance with the spiritual dimension, and, above all, it needs to be viewed as only one part of the overall practice of fellowship as it is taught in the Bible. But it is indeed a legitimate, important part of the well-rounded Christian life.

Though I cannot document it from Scripture, I believe some people have a spiritual gift that expresses itself in the area of Christian social fellowship. Perhaps it is a particular aspect of the gift of service or hospitality. In any event, these people are the ones who coordinate the church dinners or the annual Sunday school picnic, or head up the recreation time at the weekend retreat. They have a God-given knack (a gift?) for handling these activities in a way that enhances the spiritual dimension of our church or campus discipleship ministries. Their activities, when done to glorify God, are important to Him and should be to us.

As Jesus addressed the church at Laodicea, He invited them to have fellowship with Him. In that well-known passage, Revelation 3:20, Jesus said, "Here I am! I stand at the door and knock. If anyone hears my voice and opens the door, I will go in and eat with him, and he with me." In the culture of that day, to share a meal together was to have fellowship. It is quite obvious that Jesus viewed such occasions as involving more than merely a casual social relationship or a time of enjoying food and pleasant conversation together. He viewed them as an opportunity to move toward those inner circles of deeper spiritual fellowship. But in symbolically using such a social occasion to call those backslidden believers at Laodicea to repentance and restoration of fellowship, He did establish the legitimacy and the value of social fellowship in the Kingdom of God.

A final word

In this study of fellowship we have covered a wide range of topics. We have examined koinonia as the living expression of our objective relationship with God and with all other believers. We have seen that fellowship is a caring community and a partnership in the gospel, a sharing with one another spiritually and a caring for each other materially. Suffering together, serving one another, and using our spiritual gifts for the benefit of the entire Body are all conscious expressions of true biblical fellowship. With such a diversity of topics, how can we tie them all together? Is there a common thread, a single idea that will enable us to begin to apply all that we have learned intellectually about koinonia?

Yes, there is. The foundation of daily experiential fellowship among believers is found in Paul's statement that "in Christ . . . each member belongs to all the others" (Romans 12:5). I belong to you and you belong to me, and we each belong to and have "ownership" in every other believer in the world. This mutual belonging to one another is the thread that ties together all the seemingly diverse elements of fellowship. As we recognize and apply the fact that we belong to each other, we will genuinely love and care for one another. We will seek to build up one another through spiritual sharing, and we will meet each other's material needs. We will enjoy one another in times of social fellowship, and we will suffer with one another in times of trial. All of these many facets of fellowship are rooted in the concept that we belong to one another.

So let's not view all these glorious elements of New Testament koinonia as just a somewhat long list of Christian duties to be juggled precariously among all the other pressures of life. Rather, let's concentrate on this objective nature of koinonia, this belonging to one another in Christ. Then we will see these other expressions of biblical fellowship falling more naturally into place in our lives. They will not seem to be diverse, unrelated duties, but simply the appropriate responses of true koinonia to each situation and relationship we encounter. We will then begin to experience the joy of fellowship, and we will understand why those first New Testament believers "devoted themselves . . . to fellowship."